STOCK MARKET
FOR BEGINNERS
PAYCHECK FREEDOM

THE EASIEST GUIDE TO PERSONAL INVESTING EVER WRITTEN

BY DON A. SINGLETARY

Paycheck Freedom

ISBN-13: 978-1544005706
ISBN-10: 1544005709

This publication is intended to provide training information and commentary on the subjects covered. It is sold with the understanding that neither the author nor the publisher is engaged in rendering legal, accounting, or securities trading, or other professional services. If legal advice or other expert assistance is required, the services of a competent professional person should be sought.

Any stocks or trades, observations, and opinions based on real or fictitious equities, are used for illustration and teaching purposes only in this book- and are not intended to be trading advice on any specific equities or products.

About the Author

For over 25 years, the author was a corporate trainer and commodity hedge manager for major corporations and brokerage companies. Don A. Singletary's books, speaking appearances, and articles have been highly praised for their plain language and a philosophy of common sense. Some of his articles have appeared on numerous blogs as well as *Futures Magazine*, *Stocks & Commodities Magazine*, and radio guest appearances.

The author's recent best-selling publication of *Options Exposed Playbook – The Most Profitable and Popular Online Option Strategies of All Time* is becoming a popular standard for thousands of traders who value a straight-forward introduction to the methods and benefits of option trading.

An Appeal to Common Sense

When I set out to write this book for aspiring stock market investors, I realized the reason most people fail to save - is because they've been taught to put the cart before the horse; they have been ill-advised to save for retirement without considering a far more motivating and compelling reason to save and invest: Savings is for improving your life **now**, not waiting until retirement.

Financial advisors tell people that, after having a few months salary in savings, that they should spend the rest of their lives putting money towards saving for retirement.   I want you to consider something: **The people that have been telling you this, are the people who make money when you put your savings in their accounts.** And then if you need it for an emergency (other than death or disability) you will be penalized 10%. Didn't you ever wonder who got to decide to penalize you 10% to use your own money? It's such a bad idea to urge people to save and then punish them if they need to use the money.

The 75% of our people living paycheck to paycheck don't have tax problems, they have income problems! It's time to pause and reconsider. Until you can achieve paycheck freedom, which is what I call an escape from daily financial worries, better advice might be for you to keep your investments where you can use them.

You deserve to get the benefits of your investments <u>all your life</u>, not just in retirement. If you change your thinking just a little, you will find great enjoyment in personal investing. This can change your life forever. The moment you start investing, is the moment things start getting better – no matter what age you are. – the author

Table of Contents

Introduction

John Lennon said, "Life is what happens to you while you are planning it." For us to keep sending people the message that financial security is what happens after age 65, is so wrong! This is a false narrative. <u>Financial security should start as soon as possible - and last a lifetime.</u>

The Easiest Guide to Personal Investing Ever Written
What's Inside:

- This book is like modern GPS mapping to investing – get where you want to go fast with no wrong turns

- Illustrations using these popular stocks: Apple, Google, Walt Disney, McDonalds, Chevron, JP Morgan, Cracker Barrel, Johnson & Johnson, General Motors, Home Depot, Lily Drugs, AT&T/Verizon, Pepsi & Coca-Cola, Amazon, Bank of America, and more...

- Master Investor Tips of Warren Buffett and Peter Lynch

- How to Buy Stocks for Zero Commissions

- Gain the Confidence to Manage Your Money for Life

- What & How the Wealthy Teach their Children About Money

- There is nothing else you need to buy. Everything you need is here.

Why this book? What is Different about this Book?

The United States of America has a huge financial literacy problem. We live in the richest country in the world and yet, three out of four families are living paycheck to paycheck. It's like we have the largest swimming pool in the world right in our own backyard, but we can't even get wet! Why? The answer is very simple: **We've been given the wrong instructions!**

Somehow Wall Street and the financial-services industry never got the memo. They always seem to concoct the most complex "solutions" and unwieldy theories of why things happen when the simple truth is right in front of their noses. For decades, financial advisers and so-called 'thought leaders' have wrung their hands and wagged their fingers over Americans' inability to put away savings but it is they who have failed to understand one simple thing:

"You can't catch a fish with broccoli. It might be good for him, but he doesn't want it."

– Robert Skrob

Unfortunately, people are taught that the #1 major purpose of saving money should be for retirement in a 401k, IRA, or other tax-deferred account. This is so wrong, and it kills almost all incentive for most people to save.

I was once a struggling teacher, I worked overtime teaching night classes – and I had a second job building and selling computers. Time I would have rather spent with my family, was spent working hard just struggling to get by financially. I was one of those 7 of 10 families living paycheck to paycheck. The *last* thing I thought I could afford was to put money into an IRA where I couldn't touch it for another 30 to 40 years. And I was right!

Suppose you have two five-year old children in front of you, and you make each of them an offer:

For the first child, you promise a delicious cookie right now, and all they have to do is to put away their toys.

And to the second child you make this offer: "Put away your toys and in 60 years when you are 65 years old, have worked a job hard for 40 years, and then if you still have enough teeth left to chew, I will give you a whole bag of these delicious cookies."

What people are told is that it should be a priority to take money they really can't yet afford to save and put it where they can't touch it until ten to fifty years into the future. If I wanted to manufacture advice that would prevent people from achieving financial security, that's what I would tell them! What most people need now is Paycheck Freedom and the peace of mind it can bring.

The lessons in this book hold three promises for you:

1) *You will learn how choosing a good stock for your investments is as easy as finding a pair of shoes that fit.*

2) *You can buy stocks with little or no commissions and how to keep the money so you can have it available to you to use at any time – all while reinvesting your profits free.*

3) *Eliminating paycheck to paycheck finances in as little as 36 to 60 months, by creating a second income.*

The next time you watch the hit TV show *Shark Tank*, look at the row of billionaires who all started with nothing and became hugely successful. Not one of them put the first money they made into an account they couldn't touch until they were 62 years old. *They put their first money and motivation into building a better life, not a better retirement.*

The first directives of creating a degree of financial freedom are:

1) You must be motivated to make improvements to your life immediately. If you only invest for retirement, your enthusiasm will be much less than it needs to be. Align your actions with your motivations, and you are on a course for vast improvements; this is just common sense about human nature.

2) Absolutely refuse to believe that finding good investments will require a lot of time and study on your part. By the time you finish this book, you should have no doubt about your ability to invest.

Buying stock is no more complicated than purchasing a smart phone or getting the power turned on for your home or apartment. Start by computer or over the phone with as little as a couple of hundred dollars; it is completely private and takes ten or fifteen minutes. And since you will start to see rewards almost immediately, it is fun!

In the next chapter, there are at least ten stocks to consider, all household names that are already owned by millions of people. In a later chapter, read a Q&A section on how to avoid common mistakes of new investors. This is the practical guide to easy personal stock investing.

Avoid all the rhetoric and theoretical math by learning from master investors like Warren Buffett and Peter Lynch. It is easy to set up accounts for children and grandkids for almost no cost, and allow those profits to be reinvested free for life.

A Most Important Gift of All

I assume that many people reading this book either have children or will one day. I am going to show you a ridiculous example right now. *Here are three things you must never, ever teach your children:*

1. THAT SAVINGS IS DEFINED AS WHAT MONEY YOU HAVE LEFT AFTER ALL YOUR EXPENSES.

2. OPEN A BANK SAVINGS ACCOUNT AND DEPOSIT THAT SAVINGS. HAVE THEM BELIEVE THIS IS THE SAFEST PLACE TO KEEP ONE'S MONEY.

3. PROMISE THEM IF THEY WORK HARD AND REMAIN HONEST, THEY WILL ALWAYS HAVE ENOUGH MONEY- NO MATTER WHAT.

The greatest danger in the most false of all statements, is that they contain a grain of truth. Of course we should save, work hard and be honest - but none of these things by itself guarantees us any financial security. None!

The myth that prevents Americans from financial security - is that it takes a complicated special education. When you understand this simple way to receive financial rewards now, instead of thinking only of retirement, is when you become highly motivated – and you can get things done right away towards financial comfort – instead of facing a lifetime of paycheck to paycheck.

Your children should learn to look forward to investing their dollars in good companies, not to putting leftover pennies in a bank.

You are about to be introduced to some of the most widely held stocks and the reasons why millions of Americans own them. You should do your own research of course, but these are here as examples of how many household names can lead you to investing ideas. More importantly, this is the book that doesn't hit you with a barrage of unnecessary math or the task of learning extensive theory and terms before you can go into action. What is called 'a financial education' has failed to keep pace with the times we live in. Our smart phones have more computing power and memory than all the equipment used to put a man on the moon in 1969's Apollo 11 mission. Things have changed. It is no longer complicated or expensive to invest in stocks.

In the simplest terms, the promise here is not a story of soaring to extreme wealth, but a simple and sure plan that delivers people from exhausting day to day financial worries. For many individuals and families this means an end to living paycheck to paycheck, and to illustrate how to do well enough – not to allow money worries be central to everyday life. Ignore all the advertising that urges you to save most of your extra dollars for retirement; that's a plan that just isn't working for a vast majority of people.

When a friend tells you she/he is saving for retirement, just tell them you have a plan that will pay off sooner! We live in the middle of a country of opportunity and wealth, and it is only right that we can be free from a lifetime of financial struggle. You must understand how to make decisions that can deliver the freedom to enjoy the really important things in life, those things that money can't buy.

Most people who write books about stock investing mean well, but I think far too many of them are unwittingly propagating a false narrative – that it somehow is complicated and that one must study extensively before taking the plunge into stock investing. In the first 20 pages of this book, you'll learn how to identify good stocks and invest in them. I've never seen a book on stock investing that did that, so that's why I wrote this one.

Finding and investing in a few good stocks is extremely easy work. This book has extensive quotes from Warren Buffett and Peter Lynch – and you will be pleased to hear that both of them will agree that building financial freedom is not a complicated process at all. You've heard of extremely rich people who are down to Earth and who use common sense and straight talk? Well, Warren Buffett and Peter Lynch are two such people. I can tell you from personal experience that there are thousands of people just like them. These are knowledgeable people who give good advice generously. I have been fortunate enough to meet several of them. There is a section in this book to honor one of them who became my friend (See: *About Woodrow* on page 32.)

You can find your own way to financial peace of mind from the ideas and methods in this book. These things belong to all of us; I am just lucky to be one of the messengers for this good news. My hope is that you will pass this book and its message on to friends, family members, and your children - and that they all will be better for it. –the author

The USA ranks # 14 in the world In financial literacy rankings, just behind the Czech Republic. 7 of every 10 households are living paycheck-to-paycheck and struggle almost daily with financial matters. Would you say it's time for a change?

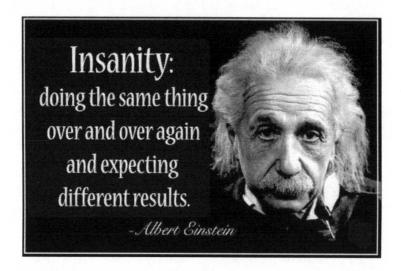

Using this book to enter the stock market is as easy as using your iPhone for directions to grandma's house.

Chapter 1
An Introduction to the Stock Market

Who Is Investing in the Stock Market?

	% Yes	% No		% Yes	% No
Total	55	45	College Grad	76	24
			Some College	44	56
Men	58	42	HS or less	23	77
Women	53	47			
			Family Income		
White	57	43	75,000 +	88	12
Black	29	71	$30k - $75k	56	44
Other	16	84	less than $30k	21	89
18-29	25	75	Registered Voters		
30-49	55	45	registered	54	46
50-64	58	42	not registered	24	76
65+	43	57			

In the table (above: *Who Is Investing in the Stock Market*?), the numbers include individuals with employer retirement/investment plans, mutual fund owners, and self-directed accounts such as types of IRA's; a great many of these people do not trade individual accounts at all. They should.

In the table **Who Is Investing in the Stock Market?**, almost everyone who sees it for the first time tries to find the categories which apply to them; this is a natural thing to do. There is one very important thing missing from this chart, but it isn't obvious to most investors. It's a piece of information that you should never, ever forget:

The stock market doesn't care who you are, what age or color you are, nor does it care whether you are registered to vote or not, or your income amount. The stock market is totally impersonal – as impersonal as gravity; it works exactly the same for everybody.

Living paycheck-to-paycheck actually costs a lot more than the inconvenience of saving small amounts on a regular basis. A lifetime of living paycheck-to-paycheck is infinitely tougher and costlier; you'll struggle and toil, not just a few years- but for decades. It won't be just you who bears this burden, but your entire family.

If it isn't there already, burn this slogan into your brain and be a responsible parent by teaching this to your children:

It is completely irrational not to save money in good investments.

Owning shares of stock is owning a small increment of an enterprise and that means sharing in the growth and/or profits of that company. Some stocks pay their shareholders some of the profits each quarter (*dividends*), and others reinvest profits into growth that will increase the value of each share of stock (often called *growth stocks*).

There are many great companies that pay shareholders dividends. These dividends are normally paid in cash every quarter. Millions of investors take advantage of what is called a DRIP, a Dividend Reinvestment Plan. You can participate in the DRIP (usually free of charge) and arrange for your broker to have the company use your dividends to buy more shares of the company instead of paying you in cash. Shares and even partial shares are bought with your dividends. This way your money is reinvested in the company free, and the money you earn begins to earn even more money faster. Just to be clear, having your dividends reinvested in a stock you own is accomplished by one phone call to your broker, that's it! You don't have to do any more than that.

Here's how investing in McDonalds (MCD) for only 13 years would have accumulated with a base investment (initial buy) of $1,000:

```
STOCK TOTAL RETURN CALCULATOR

Stock Ticker:    MCD              Starting Amount ($):  1000

Starting Date:   12/28/2002      Ending Date:          01/2/2016

RESULTS

Total Amount :   $10,908.39       Annualized Return:  20.14%
```

Had you decided to add $25 a week more during those 13 years, instead of $10,908, you would have made so much more, about $65,008.

```
STOCK TOTAL RETURN CALCULATOR

Stock Ticker:    MCD              Starting Amount ($):  1000

Starting Date:   12/28/2002      Ending Date:          01/2/2016

            Calculate     Reset

ADVANCED OPTIONS

    • Only touch these if you want to model adding money to the account periodically.
    • By default, only dividends will be reinvested.

Reinvestment ($):   25            Frequency:  Every Week

RESULTS

Total Amount :   $65,008.43       Annualized Return:  17.31%
```

These two windows of calculation are from a free online calculator; you can find and use it at: http://dqydj.com/stock-return-calculator-dividend-reinvestment-drip/ Our thanks to Don't Quit Your Day Job **dqydj.com**

The following is from: Dividend.Com at: http://www.dividend.com/dividend-investing-101/dividend-reinvestment-plans-drips/

The Results of Reinvesting Dividends

Over the long term, enrolling stock in a DRIP plan can increase the value of an initial investment substantially. Below are two examples of how a DRIP program could have benefited investors in the past.

If you had $2,000 invested in Pepsi in 1980, that would be worth more than $150,000 by the end of 2004. You would have started with 80 shares, but by reinvesting dividends, you'd now have 2,800 shares.

If you had $2,000 invested in Philip Morris in 1980, that would be worth just under $300,000 by the end of 2004. You would have started with 58 shares. Today, thanks to stock splits and reinvesting dividends, you now would have more than 4,300 shares.

It is not only a free service but it is a regular habit of many investors to have the dividends, the company shared profits, reinvested for stockholders. Talk to your broker about arranging this (usually free) service. Remember this is called DRIP.

When financial writers, sellers of systems, and journalist go back in time to pick the very best money-making examples – some of the results are not typical as those of an average investor, but still they can be remarkable. Here's an example, though admittedly this is 'cherry picking':

If an investor had invested $1,000 and added only $50 per week in Amazon (AMZN), here are the results:

Total invested: $1,000 + $50 per week in Amazon stock

10 years: November 1996 – November 2016: $162,509
5 years: November 2011 – November 2016: $ 32,828

In only five years, this investor would have accomplished this:

- NOT EVER LIVING PAYCHECK TO PAYCHECK AGAIN.

- ALWAYS HAVING CASH FOR EMERGENCIES AND FAMILY NEEDS

- A GREAT START ON A LONG-TERM NEST EGG FOR HER/HIS FAMILY

Not setting out to accomplish these three simple things, is the most irrational decision a person can make. Not spending more than you earn and investing a modest sum for these simple financial freedoms is all it takes – and yet as many as 75% families never do it.

The Best News of All about Investing in the Stock Market

Here are some facts that will bust many myths about stock investing. For many people, this will be a 're-booting' of everything you think you know about stock investments. If you have common sense, the information in the next few paragraphs could be the most motivating and empowering thing you may ever learn about personal investing. All of the following statements are FALSE:

- I NEED TO SPEND AT LEAST TWO HOURS A WEEK OR MORE TO MANAGEMENT MY INVESTMENTS AND PICK STOCKS.

- I WON'T BE ABLE TO INVEST WISELY UNTIL I LEARN A LOT ABOUT THE STOCK MARKET.

- I NEED TO READ MORE BOOKS OR TAKE A COURSE ON INVESTING IN STOCKS BEFORE I BUY STOCKS.

- THERE ARE SO MANY PEOPLE THAT CAN INVEST BETTER THAN I CAN.

- I WILL NEED A LOT OF HELP, PERHAPS AN ADVISORY SERVICE OR FINANCIAL PLANNER, IN ORDER TO BE SMART ABOUT INVESTMENTS.

Most people will tell you that these five statements are true but remember, 75% of those people giving you that advice are living paycheck to paycheck! Just because a large group of people agree, doesn't make them right. Perhaps you've heard the story of "The Emperor's Clothes"; if not, here is a quick refresher for you.

*"**The Emperor's New Clothes**" is a short tale by Hans Christian Andersen about two weavers who promise an emperor a new suit of clothes. The story goes like this:*

A vain Emperor who cares about nothing except wearing and displaying clothes hires two weavers who promise him the finest, best suit of clothes from a fabric invisible to anyone who is unfit for his position or "hopelessly stupid". The Emperor's ministers cannot see the clothes themselves, but pretend that they can for fear of appearing unfit for their positions and the Emperor does the same. Finally the weavers report that the suit is finished, they mime dressing him and the Emperor marches in procession before his subjects. The townsfolk play along with the pretense, not

wanting to appear unfit for their positions or stupid. Then a child in the crowd, too young to understand the desirability of keeping up the pretense, blurts out that the Emperor is wearing nothing at all and the cry is taken up by others. The Emperor suspects the assertion is true but continues the procession.

Anyone who tells you that you don't know enough and/or lack the experience or knowledge to buy some stock, is telling you "the Emperor's clothes look great!" After reading this book, most people are quite capable of opening an account and purchasing stock shares – and doing it comfortably.

Unless you already have a high net worth, various investments with tax ramifications, and classes of assets and property in your life – you won't need anything more than common sense to get started. To prove this, I present this table (below). This table presents the 20-year results of a modest investment of only a thousand dollars, adding either $50 or $100 per week during the investment period. The eight stocks presented in the table are common household names and brands. Virtually everyone who doesn't live in a cave knows about these companies. Each of these eight stocks are widely owned and traded in relatively high volume; they are owned by millions of individuals, by retirement plans, insurance companies, investment houses, mutual funds, ETF's (exchange traded funds), public & private trust funds, and by millions of people all around the world. Some very savvy and knowledgeable investors hold shares of these stocks right now.

Stock Market Twenty Year Investments from January 1996 - January 2016

Symbol	Name	Starting with $1000 and $50 per Week		Starting with $1000 and $100 per Week	
		TOTAL	Annual Return	TOTAL	Annual Return
AFL	Aflac	$152,348	9.43%	$293,286	9.27%
JNJ	Johnson & Johnson	$148,277	9.20%	$288,916	9.15%
PEP	Pepsico	$143,769	8.91%	$280,623	8.90%
CPB	Campbell Soup	$112,337	6.85%	$221,571	6.87%
XOM	Exxon	$120,870	7.47%	$235,332	7.39%
WFC	Wells Fargo	$174,565	10.55%	$338,011	10.46%
WMT	Wal-mart	$104,007	6.18%	$209,775	6.01%
MCD	McDonalds	$229,623	12.79%	$451,353	12.84%

ALL DIVIDENDS REINVESTED AS STOCK SHARES WHEN APPLICABLE

These stock shares represent stalwart businesses, have multi-year track records, good reputations, long histories of good performance, and the outlook for them to perform in the future is, in varying degrees, good to great. I could have easily made this list with 50 stocks or more. The point here is that you don't need to be an expert to find plenty of companies that are good investments. And don't forget, the free stock profits calculator at dqydj.com

This is NOT a retirement plan. This is something that can be done now to begin to improve a person's financial position. It just isn't "rocket science" to find a good stock to start building your personal wealth. There is no need to "reinvent the wheel" in order to take advantage of widely available knowledge. You don't need your own stock guru, financial planner, or financial expert to find some great investments. There is no need for you to take two hours a week on your trading account. It only takes one or two good stocks to start. There is no great mystery or long educational process that you must perform before you start. Anyone that tells you any different, even though they may be well-intentioned, is only parroting misinformation. Get started now and over time, you will learn more as you go.

Already, just in the first chapter of this book, you have two great web links where you can check on almost any stock's performance in any time period you choose. There are a few tables in this book (one of them above here) that feature stocks worthy of your consideration. It is extremely important that you see how simple it really is to select good stocks for long-term profits. Equally important is 'what not to do' and there is plenty of information about that in the chapters ahead.

Just yesterday, a friend phoned me and told me about a stock that could make a fortune. This stock is one of the marijuana start-up stocks and only sells for 15 cents ($0.15) per share. He may as well have been telling me to go buy a lotto ticket. There are many similar start-up stocks right now as drug laws change - but trying to guess which two or three of them might be dominate in their industry five, ten, or fifteen years from now – is as difficult as guessing the ranking of the twelve top NFL teams in order for a season. Almost impossible.

Why do people buy these (very inexpensive) so-called *penny stocks*? The same reason they buy a lotto ticket: Even though they know they will almost certainly lose, it is fun to think of fantastic possibilities for a short nearby period of time. Any time someone offers you something for nothing (or very nearly nothing), grab your wallet and run the other way!

Anyone who has ever watched *Shark Tank* will tell you that it isn't 'good ideas' that make money; it is the planning, execution, and timing of good business practices that succeed. Don't mistake lotto ticket odds for good investments. The old adage "if it sounds too good to be true, it probably is," is a truth every good, common-sense investor understands. I don't really need to tell you this; you already know it. You don't bet your financial fate and security on long shots. There are plenty of 'success stories' that you will hear to tempt you into risky investments; just remember most people who invested in gold claims died miserably poor, but the ones that got lucky always attracted scores of others into the game. Until you accumulate enough money to become financially sound, stay on the sure and steady track. By then you might be able to venture into higher risk/higher return with a small portion of your wealth. Make financial security your first goal for you and your family.

If you've ever been to a casino with slot machines, you have noticed the ones that win make lots of flashy lights and noise, but all the losers are silent!

In the coming chapters, you will learn to choose a broker, open an account, and how to practice without risking real money. Coming up in the next chapter, *The Basics of Stocks,* you will learn about the exchanges and types of stocks available.

"Never depend on a single income. Make investments to create a second source."

"Someone is sitting in the shade today because someone planted a tree long ago."

"Do not save what is left after spending but spend what is left after saving."

Chapter 2: The Basics of Stocks

There's more about him later in this chapter. Here's a quote from Peter Lynch, perhaps one of the most successful stock buyers in the world:

Everyone has the brainpower to follow the stock market. If you made it through fifth-grade math, you can do it. - Peter Lynch

When you buy a share of a company, you own a tiny bit of it. So you are, in effect, going into business with that company. When people think investing is out of their league because they don't have a lot of money or knowledge, it's a huge mistake. With certificates of deposit paying around 3%, and the S&P 500 stocks averaging about 10%, you can see how you almost have to invest in stocks over the long haul to make any money.

It will take a 3% yield almost 24 years to double. With a 10% average yield it will only take about 7.2 years to double.

Did You Know? The day before the ex-dividend date of a dividend-paying stock is the last day of ownership (of record) before the next dividend payout. Dividends are paid usually each quarter. You don't have to own the stock for the whole quarter (or any specific length of time) to get the dividend, you simply must own it on the day before the ex-dividend date to get this payout. Ask your broker or shareholder services for more information.

One of the things that stops a lot of people from investing is the belief that they don't have enough money to buy several stocks, so they won't *have all their eggs in one basket*.   They are told, falsely, that the only way to invest safely is to diversify. Many people are dissuaded by this false advice, so instead they put off investing at all – a big mistake!

There is a basis for this thought - but as is the case with so many well-derived pieces of research, it gets dumbed-down and shortened into media bites of so-called sound advice that go viral and are repeated by generations until they become 'conventional wisdom' without any further discussion of whether it is really good advice or not.

The source of 'safety in diversity' also known as *modern portfolio theory* (MPT), was introduced by economist Harry Markowitz in a 1952 essay for which he was later awarded a one-third share of the Nobel Prize in economics in 1959. His work on *efficient diversification* was adapted as a standard *theory* in the field of financial portfolio management.

I hope I don't need to point out the irony that something done in 1952 is still named *modern* portfolio theory. His theory may have been the best or most modern at that time, but times have changed. We all know how quickly in the information age, the 'best things' so easily get replaced with 'better things.'

There is a very popular investor who has ignored this advice (MPT) for years and is one of the best investors and richest people in the world, Warren Buffett. There are some good books on how he does it and well-worth the read, but I am going to share, in my own words, what I believe to be the essence of this genius investor. What I admire most about Warren Buffett is that what he does is little more than common sense and quite logical, and yet it goes against virtually every money manager that urges people to diversify widely to avoid risks. I'll explain it right now in simple language and you make up your own mind:

If you owned a stable of 100 thoroughbred race horses, and 10% of them won 95% of the races, why would you enter all 100 or even 80 of them in the races? You wouldn't! And that, my friend, is how easy it is to show you the essence of good investing. There is a current day movement among modern managers that is ditching the long-held - and perhaps overly simplistic view- of safety in diversification – and it's about time. This doesn't negate investing in various *kinds* of assets for safety, but if you are going to put money in stocks, you might want a very few good ones instead of buying 100 with a shotgun approach. And starting with only one or two stocks is infinitely better than doing nothing!

The Major Exchanges

The trading software, called your *trading platform*, furnished by your broker performs many functions. One of those functions is *routing* your orders to buy/sell to the correct exchange so it can be *executed*. This all happens transparently.

The New York Stock Exchange (abbreviated as **NYSE** and nicknamed "The Big Board"), is an American stock exchange in Lower Manhattan, New York City. It is by far the world's largest stock exchange by market capitalization of its listed companies at US$19.3 trillion as of June 2016. The average daily trading value was approximately US$169 billion in 2013. The NYSE is owned by Intercontinental Exchange, an American holding company that it also lists (NYSE: ICE). Previously, it was part of NYSE Euronext (NYX), which was formed by the NYSE's 2007 merger with Euronext. NYSE and Euronext now operate as divisions of Intercontinental Exchange.

American Stock Exchange: NYSE MKT LLC, formerly known as the American Stock Exchange (**AMEX**), is an American stock exchange situated in New York City, New York. AMEX was previously a mutual organization, owned by its members. On January 17, 2008, NYSE Euronext announced it would acquire the AMEX for $260 million in stock; on October 1, 2008, NYSE Euronext completed the acquisition. Before the closing of the acquisition, NYSE Euronext announced that the AMEX would be integrated with the Alternext European small-cap exchange and renamed the NYSE Alternext U.S.

The **Nasdaq Stock Market** (**NASDAQ**) is an American stock exchange- and the second-largest exchange in the world by market capitalization, behind only the New York Stock Exchange.

CBOE: Chicago Board Option Exchange The world's largest market for options on stocks, indexes, and interest rates.

CME: Chicago Mercantile Exchange The country's largest futures exchange, and the second largest in the world. New York Mercantile Exchange (**NYMEX**): The NYMEX is the world's largest physical commodity futures exchange, offering exposure to a wide variety of products. Commodity Exchange Inc. (**COMEX**) also operates as a division of the NYMEX and is best known for offering exposure to various metals contracts.

As you learn stock investing and sound financial principles, there will be things that are *nice to know,* and things you *need to know.* This information on all the exchanges is *nice* to know. The good news is that all you *need* to know, is that your software will automatically route your orders to the proper exchanges.

Stock Market Indicators

DJIA: Dow Jones Industrial Average, also called The Dow, DOW, DOW 30, Industrial Average. It is an index that shows how 30 large publicly owned companies based in the United States have traded during a standard trading session in the stock market.

MMM 3M	**INTC** Intel
AXP American Express	**JNJ** Johnson & Johnson
AAPL Apple	**JPM** JPMorgan Chase
BA Boeing	**MCD** McDonald's
CAT Caterpillar	**MRK** Merck
CVX Chevron	**MSFT** Microsoft
CSCO Cisco	**NKE** Nike
KO Coca-Cola	**PFE** Pfizer
DIS Disney	**PG** Procter & Gamble
DD E I du Pont de Nemours and Co	**TRV** Travelers Companies Inc
XOM Exxon Mobil	**UTX** United Technologies
GE General Electric	**UNH** UnitedHealth
GS Goldman Sachs	**VZ** Verizon
HD Home Depot	**V** Visa
IBM IBM	**WMT** Wal-Mart

S&P 500: The Standard & Poor's 500, often abbreviated as the S&P 500, or just "the S&P" is an American stock market index based on the market capitalizations of 500 large companies having common stock listed on the NYSE or NASDAQ. The S&P 500 index components and their weightings are determined by S&P Dow Jones Indices. It differs from other U.S. stock market indices, such as the Dow Jones Industrial Average or the Nasdaq Composite index because of its diverse constituency and weighting methodology. It is one of the most commonly followed equity indices, and many consider it one of the best representations of the U.S. stock market, and a bellwether for the U.S. economy.

There are many indicators of the stock market's performance, far too many to name here – and there are dozens of indexes of various *sectors* of the markets such as energy, pharmaceuticals, manufacturing, technology, and so on. Some of these indicators or indexes are called *broad market indicators* because they have a larger size sample, like the Russell 2000 – an index based on the prices of 2000 stock prices. There are ways to trade these indexes as individual securities in your portfolio including futures on the indexes, ETF (Exchange Traded Funds), mutual funds, options, hedge funds, and managed investments.

If you are beginning, avoid information overload. Just know for now, that there are dozens and even hundreds of specialized stocks and funds for market segments, categories, and other groupings. **The Exchange Traded Funds or ETF's** can offer both tax efficiency and lower transaction costs. More than two trillion dollars have been invested in ETFs since they were first introduced in the United States in 1993. By the end of 2016, ETFs offer more than 2000 different products, covering almost every conceivable market sector, niche and trading strategy. ETF's are listed on the exchanges just like shares of stock and are traded the same as stock shares. ETF's can be a very efficient way to either diversify or specialize your investments. For example, some mirror the DOW 30, precious metals like gold, and other sectors and specialties like dividends, energy, and technology.

Did you Know? The symbol for an Exchange traded fund that trades the S&P 500 Index is SPY. The symbol for an ETF that trades the NASDAQ 100 index is QQQ. If you are giving thought to using such an ETF in lieu of buying individual stocks, you should do your homework to see which, if any, might be suitable for you. Shares are traded just like stock shares on the stock exchanges.

Amazon Bigger than Wal-mart

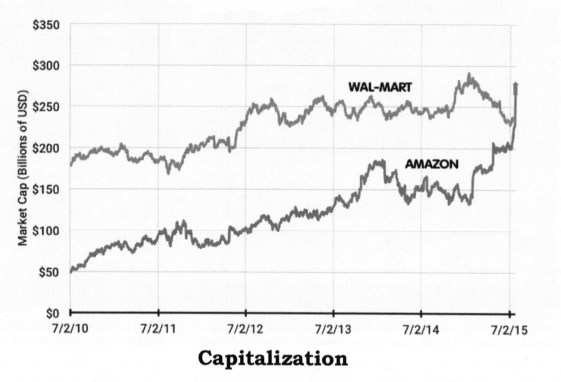

Capitalization

The market capitalization of a stock is the value of all of its outstanding shares. Viewing capitalization allows comparisons and evaluations of a company and its shares.

Big-cap or large cap refers to a company with a market capitalization value of more than $5 billion. Large cap is a shortened version of the term *large market capitalization*. (50 largest in table as of 11/2016)

Small cap stocks are not actually that small. *Small cap* refers to the market capitalization of a company. While the range can vary depending on who you ask, small cap refers to a company with a market capitalization between $200 million and $2.5 billion.

Each stock exchange has its respective requirements for listing a stock. Stocks that either do not meet an exchange's requirements or have (in some cases) chosen not to do so, are traded OTC. OTC means Over-The-Counter, not on a major exchange.

Some Popular Dividend Paying Stocks

When considering stocks that pay dividends, please know that the best picks are not the stocks that pay the highest dividends. Some companies might be offering very high dividend returns and it can be a sign that something is wrong. For example, in an environment when good dependable stocks like General Motors, Verizon, and Coca-Cola are paying 3% to 4%, and you see a company with a dividend of 20% or 30%, you can almost bet the company is in trouble of some kind. Stay away; if it sounds too good to be true it probably is; a dividend that high will carry a high risk of you losing your money.

Here's what you want to insist on when you shop for dividend paying stocks:

✓ A long standing track record with a quality company.

✓ A long-term history of consistency in paying good rates of return.

✓ Even companies that are not paying the highest dividends can have attractive growth rates, so you may want to consider the combined (growth & dividends) rates of return.

✓ Be aware that dividend rates can be cyclical. For

Rank	Company Name	Symbol	Market Cap ($B)
1	Apple	AAPL	596.1
2	Alphabet Inc.	GOOG	529.55
3	Microsoft	MSFT	470.64
4	Berkshire Hathaway	BRK-A	389.16
5	Amazon	AMZN	370.81
6	Exxon Mobil	XOM	361.26
7	Facebook	FB	346.96
8	Johnson & Johnson	JNJ	310.49
9	JPMorgan Chase	JPM	282.04
10	General Electric	GE	278.13
11	Wells Fargo	WFC	264.27
12	AT&T	T	240.79
13	Procter & Gamble	PG	223.34
14	Wal-Mart	WMT	220.33
15	Bank of America	BAC	210.79
16	Chevron	CVX	209.54
17	Verizon Communications	VZ	206.56
18	Pfizer	PFE	192.31
19	Coca-Cola	KO	179.12
20	Merck	MRK	171.52
21	Visa	V	169.32
22	Intel	INTC	167.95
23	Comcast	CMCSA	165.49
24	Oracle	ORCL	165.33
25	Home Depot	HD	162.56
26	Citigroup	C	161.81
27	Disney	DIS	158.81
28	IBM	IBM	155.12
29	Cisco Systems	CSCO	151.24
30	PepsiCo	PEP	146.53
31	UnitedHealth Group	UNH	145.45
32	Philip Morris International	PM	138.52
33	Altria	MO	125.75
34	Mastercard Inc.	MA	115.21
35	Schlumberger	SLB	113.1
36	Amgen	AMGN	108.19
37	Medtronic	MDT	104.36
38	3M	MMM	104.35
39	United Parcel Service	UPS	101.45
40	Kraft Heinz Co	KHC	100.97
41	QUALCOMM	QCOM	100.86
42	McDonald's	MCD	100.2
43	Gilead Sciences	GILD	99.39
44	AbbVie Inc.	ABBV	98.34
45	Bristol-Myers Squibb	BMY	95.23
46	Celgene	CELG	93.85
47	Boeing	BA	92.6
48	Walgreens Boots Alliance	WBA	91.46
49	United Technologies	UTX	89.57
50	Goldman Sachs	GS	88.53

example, companies that deal with precious metals or oil can have long multi-year cycles of rise and falling prices.

✓ Some stocks have stellar histories of paying rising dividends for decades; don't just study a one or two year history, think long-term.

Here's a representative list of some good dividend stocks*:

American Express (AXP): 1.8% dividend yield

Apple (AAPL): 2.1% dividend yield

U.S. Bancorp (USB): 2.3% dividend yield

Kinder Morgan (KMI): 2.3% dividend yield

Deere & Company (DE): 2.6% dividend yield

United Parcel Service (UPS): 2.7% dividend yield

Johnson & Johnson (JNJ): 2.8% dividend yield

Wells Fargo & Company (WFC): 2.9% dividend yield

The Kraft Heinz Company (KHC): 2.9% dividend yield

Wal-Mart (WMT): 2.9% dividend yield

General Electric (GE): 3.0% dividend yield

Phillips 66 (PSX): 3.0% dividend yield

Procter & Gamble (PG): 3.3% dividend yield

Coca-Cola (KO): 3.4% dividend yield

IBM (IBM): 3.5% dividend yield

Sanofi (SNY): 4.2% dividend yield

General Motors (GM): 4.6% dividend yield

Verizon (VZ): 4.8% dividend yield

*This list is as of NOV 2016. There are many good choices not included in this list. Such lists in this book are not intended to be investment advice but are representative examples, illustrations for guidance only.

You should notice as you peruse this dividend-paying stock list that all of these companies are large cap stocks, recognizable names with long-term records of performance, and they all are traded in high volume and followed by most major analysts. It is easy for a personal investor to find reliable and up-to-date information on such widely held stocks. It is always good when researching a stock to consult several sources. Generally speaking, even when there is a story about how a stock is 'hot', go back and consult analysts' findings. Opinions expressed in 'story-of-the-day' articles on blogs/TV may not be reliable indicators on a stocks performance. Often many commentators on financial channels will be speaking to investors who are willing to take higher risk or shorter term gains. Stay with steady and reliable.

Price-to-Earnings Ratio, Price-to-Sales, and Book Value

P/E is short for the ratio of a company's share price to its per-share earnings. As the name implies, to calculate the P/E, you simply take the current stock price of a company and divide by its earnings per share (EPS):

$$\text{P/E Ratio} = \frac{\text{Market Value per Share}}{\text{Earnings per Share}}$$

Normally, the P/E is calculated using EPS from the last four quarters. This is also known as the *trailing* P/E. The *leading* P/E is the projected earnings over the next four quarters. There is a hybrid P/E when the last two and next two quarters' estimate are used.

When studying a stock, it is the normal practice to compare its P/E with stocks of the same sector. This way you can see how a stock's price compares with other companies in the same or similar business. For example, it is pretty useless to compare a utility company stock's P/E with the P/E of a stock that is not the same type of business; one would compare the P/E of a utility stock with other utility stocks, not retailers or pharmaceuticals, etc.

A stock's **Price-to-Sales (PS) ratio** reflects how much investors are paying for each dollar of revenues generated by the company. If the Price-to-Sales ratio is 1, it means that you're paying $1 for every $1 of revenues generated by the company. The lower the **PS ratio,** the better.

Price-to-Earnings (P/E) ratio is the most common and widely used valuation metric. The Price-to-Sales ratio may become more relevant for evaluating companies with losses, or companies during a cycle of development, while generating little or no profit. On a chart a decreasing PS ratio could be a sign of recovery. The PS, when compared to other stocks in the same sector/category can be an indicator of a company's relative valuation (overpriced or underpriced in its sector.)

Investors should be aware that Price-to-Earnings of a company are always subject to accounting estimates and management manipulation, and might reflect on internal priorities in a company. For example, a company could have high debt service expenses that lower profit margins, even though sales may be high. Some companies often create more shares and sell them to service or pay off debt; this *dilutes* the outstanding shares making them worth less at shareholders expense. Conversely, when a company does a share *buy back*, they purchase shares of their stock and this increases the value of outstanding shares (the opposite of share *dilution.*) It is good news for shareholders when a company *buys back* its shares.

Amazon (AMZN) has been rapidly expanding by investing its profits into building more distribution centers, an expensive process. Because of this, the company - in some quarters - reflects a lower EPS (earnings per share), but this reinvestment increases the future or potential value of the company. This is an example of how a stock may report lower EPS while increasing its value and potential earnings. Also, there are companies (like many utility companies) that choose to pay dividends; this can reduce EPS but still keep the stock attractive to investors. The point here is while EPS is a great indicator, it does not necessarily tell the whole story of a stock's health or potential.

The **book value** is the value of a stock asset according to its balance sheet account balance. Traditionally, a company's book value is its total assets minus intangible assets and liabilities. However, in practice, depending on the source of the calculation, book value may variably include goodwill, intangible assets, or both. The value inherent in its workforce, part of the Intellectual capital of a company, is always ignored. When intangible assets and goodwill are explicitly excluded, the metric is often specified to be *tangible book value.*

In the United Kingdom, the term *net asset value* may refer to the book value of a company.

You'll be able to get complete information, quotes and news on your online broker's website. For now, so you can see how easy it is to find information on stocks and to look up some of the terms just discussed here, you can go to **www.wikinvest.com**, sign up free and explore. It used to take hours to find all this information, now it only takes milliseconds- and it's free.

Information Overload and KISS

Whether you are a seasoned veteran or a beginner in stock trading, there is one piece of advice that is valuable above all others. It was spoken by mentor and pupil, from Benjamin Graham to Warren Buffett:

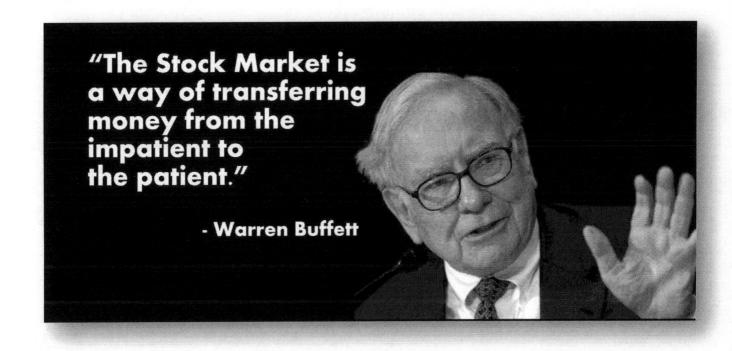

"The Stock Market is a way of transferring money from the impatient to the patient."

- Warren Buffett

Benjamin Graham born Benjamin Grossbaum; (May 9, 1894 – September 21, 1976) was a British-born American economist and professional investor. Graham is considered the father of value investing, an investment approach he began teaching at Columbia Business School in 1928 and subsequently refined with David Dodd through various editions of their famous book *Security Analysis*. Graham had many disciples in his lifetime, a number of whom went on to become successful investors themselves. Perhaps the most well-known is Warren Buffett. Buffett credits Graham as grounding him with a sound intellectual investment framework, and described Graham as the second most influential person in his life after his own father. Graham wrote that investment is most intelligent when it is most businesslike. By that he meant that the stock investor is neither right nor wrong because others agreed or disagreed with him; he is right because his facts and analysis are right.

Warren Buffett is legendary for using the principles of value investing, his patience and savvy, and his frugality with a common-sense approach. If you aren't familiar with his life and accomplishments, it is worth your time to Google him.

WARREN EDWARD BUFFETT; BORN AUGUST 30, 1930, IS AN AMERICAN BUSINESS MAGNATE, INVESTOR AND PHILANTHROPIST. HE IS CONSIDERED BY SOME TO BE ONE OF THE MOST SUCCESSFUL INVESTORS IN THE WORLD. BUFFETT IS THE CHAIRMAN, CEO AND LARGEST SHAREHOLDER OF BERKSHIRE HATHAWAY, AND IS CONSISTENTLY RANKED AMONG THE WORLD'S WEALTHIEST PEOPLE. HE WAS RANKED AS THE WORLD'S WEALTHIEST PERSON IN 2008 AND AS THE THIRD WEALTHIEST IN 2015. IN 2012 *TIME* NAMED BUFFETT ONE OF THE WORLD'S MOST INFLUENTIAL PEOPLE. (SOURCE: WIKIPEDIA)

This chart gives you a lifelong history of his investment value method results:

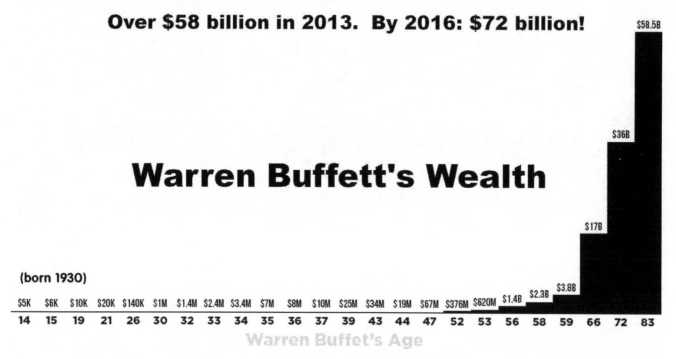

Over $58 billion in 2013. By 2016: $72 billion!

Warren Buffett's Wealth

(born 1930)

$5K	$6K	$10K	$20K	$140K	$1M	$1.4M	$2.4M	$3.4M	$7M	$8M	$10M	$25M	$34M	$19M	$67M	$376M	$620M	$1.4B	$2.3B	$3.8B	$17B	$36B	$58.5B
14	15	19	21	26	30	32	33	34	35	36	37	39	43	44	47	52	53	56	58	59	66	72	83

Warren Buffet's Age

My reasons for illustrating Buffett's steady-as-she-goes methods are simple. As a new investor, or any investor really - one must gather a sound foundation to build upon. A personal investment philosophy, with patience and consistency are a must for success. You have every incentive to design and protect your own methods and work ethic, otherwise you are left with nothing but inconsistent chancy guesses. If you follow those who profess an easy, fast, and totally safe path to riches, then you are foolish and this will only add space between you and the achievement of personal wealth.

30

No matter what the talent or the efforts, some things just take time. You can't produce a baby in a month by getting nine women pregnant. - W. B.

When someone tells you there is no risk in a method to make you rich that only takes 10 minutes a week, put your hand over your wallet and run, don't walk, the other way. – the author

What is the most common mistake in trading?

This is a no-brainer and you already know all about it, but it might be good for you to hear it again – that's up to you. The most common mistake in trading is also the most common mistaking in living. We take our profits too quickly and let the losses run until we lose a lot. This is not only the worst mistake of investors but also the most common – and one of the hardest to cure. If you want to avoid it and you don't have an iron-strong self-discipline and a photographic memory – then you need to learn to apply discipline to your trading. This means keeping notes and records of how you are doing, so you can look at the results somewhat objectively. Doing this without fail - will help you learn faster with fewer mistakes.

You cannot manage your investments unless you can manage your emotions.

The reason for this most common mistake is that we must admit we were wrong to close a trade which we probably thought was a sure winner. We are put in a position to disagree with ourselves, a position that all of us naturally try to avoid. This is self-denial at its worst; we must remember everyone has losing trades, disappointing trades, and there are times we don't recognize our mistakes until we have already entered a trade – and then irrational thinking can take over and increase what would have been tolerable losses. Every great warrior with a long career knows he or she has to sometimes retreat to be able to fight another day. Keeping your money is just as important as making it. We normally like to think of ourselves as having a positive outlook and a life full of hope. Not learning to cut your losses, admit when a trade isn't working, and accepting the fact that you can't control everything - can lead to a quick end to your trading. Insisting on being hopeful on trades when, over a fair amount of time, a stock isn't performing - is a very bad habit – and it gets very expensive.

Almost all the time, you just let your long-term stocks ride the normal up's and down's of the market. One of the most wonderful things about trading is that it is solitary and we live and die on our own wits; that is also the worst thing about trading. For most traders, the most difficult time for discipline is when choosing stocks to buy.

About Woodrow

Back in the 1980's, before the internet and personal computers, and long before online trading – I was a stock broker for about a year. Patty and I had just had our second child and I gave up a perfectly great job in the Florida Department of Commerce's Division of Economic Development. I quit the job because I was traveling over seventy percent of the time; the job required it, but I was ready to get off the road and be at home. A good friend had told me that while handling people's money, I would learn a lot about them. This was an understatement. Being a broker gave me a 'front row seat' into people's motivations and attitudes about money, greed, fear, and ambition.

But there was one client I had who taught me more about investing than all the others put together, Woodrow. His almost innate knack to constantly pick winners amazed me and all who knew him. He was in his 70's, in good health, and worth tens of millions of dollars. Yet he dressed modestly, was extraordinarily kind and courteous -, and he came by the office about four mornings a week, usually half an hour before the market opened for the day. In those days, there was a stock quote machine in the lobby and half a dozen copies of the Wall Street Journal, free coffee, and a few other papers and magazines for our customers. Woodrow's wife had passed, his kids all grown and moved away. There is a quote from

Warren Buffett's right-hand man, Charlie Munger, that always reminds me of Woodrow and his genius for investing with simple, unassuming, common-sense:

> *"It is remarkable how people like us (he and Mr. Buffett) have gotten so much long-term advantage by consistently trying to be not stupid instead of trying to be very intelligent."*

One Tuesday morning, Woodrow came by, read the WSJ, and then poked his head in my office door and said, "I'm going to run over to that new store in town and get a few things, and I'll be back soon to sit down with you."

He left, but returned in only ten minutes and came into my office and sat down. I said to him, "That was a quick trip; didn't expect you back so soon."

He said, "Heck, I couldn't even find a parking place they were so busy. How much are the shares for that Walmart company?"

This was Spring of 1987. I gave Woodrow the quote, "$3.64 a share."

"Then buy me 10,000 shares," was the order for me to execute.

I recall another day when Woodrow walked in and came straight to my office. He said good morning and got a cup of coffee then sat down. I knew he had something on his mind, so I waited for him to speak.

"You know, if a fella can't make a phone call or buy himself a Coca-Cola, it won't matter how much money he has because it won't be worth anything, don't you think?" I agreed. This was just before the Baby Bell breakup of ATT, and Coca-Cola was $2.80 a share. He already owned both stocks, but doubled up on them that day by purchasing a few thousand shares of each.

Look back up the page and read that quote from Charlie Munger again, and you'll know exactly why it reminds me of my late friend, Woodrow.

There was one other thing about Woodrow that is forever indelible in my memory and it has nothing to do with money. One morning when he stepped into my office, he reached into his pocket and pulled out a diamond wedding band. It was simple and had one spectacular diamond in it. He held it out for me to examine, and he said, "This was her (his late wife's) wedding ring. None of my kids need it, and I never thought of selling it because I wouldn't need to. I don't know what it's worth."

"It's beautiful," I said as Woodrow looked it over again and put it back into his pocket. Even though Woodrow was worth something north of $50 million, I knew beyond any doubt that he would have parted with all of it for just one more day with his wife.

Invest in What You Know

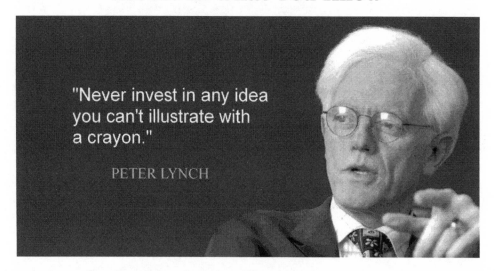

"Never invest in any idea you can't illustrate with a crayon."

PETER LYNCH

Peter Lynch (born January 19, 1944) is an American businessman and stock investor. As the manager of the Magellan Fund at Fidelity Investments between 1977 and 1990, Lynch averaged a 29.2% annual return, consistently more than doubling the S&P 500 market index and making it the best performing mutual fund in the world. During his tenure, assets under management increased from $18 million to $14 billion. He also co-authored a number of books and papers on investing.

As I look back on it now, it's obvious that studying history and philosophy was much better preparation for the stock market than, say, studying statistics. All the math you need in the stock market you get in the fourth grade. - Peter Lynch

His most famous investment principle is simply, "Invest in what you know," popularizing the economic concept of "local knowledge." Since most people tend to become expert in certain fields, applying this basic "invest in what you know" principle helps individual investors find good investments. He would ask his wife and kids what the most popular fads were and then investigate the companies behind the products. Peter Lynch wrote two books: *One Up On Wall Street* (1989) and *Beating the Street* (1993) which demonstrated his investment philosophy and approach to investing in stocks.

> *Lynch found some of his best ideas when he was out with his family, traveling or talking with friends and associates. As one famous story goes, one day his wife excitedly told him how much she liked L'eggs pantyhose, a new product she'd just tried out. After looking into the company's prospects and liking what he saw, Lynch bought the Hanes Company, maker of L'eggs, and his fund investors realized a 30-fold appreciation in Hanes stock.* (author note: Remember Woodrow couldn't find a parking place at Walmart!)

Lynch uses this principle as a starting point for investors. He has also often said that the individual investor is more capable of making money from stocks than a fund manager because they are able to spot good investments in their day-to-day lives before Wall Street. Throughout his two classic investment primers, he has outlined many of the investments he found when not in his office. He found them when he was out with his family, driving around or making a purchase at the mall.

I've included some quotes attributed to Mr. Lynch below. I've always loved quotes as they are easy to remember and can often have much wisdom condensed down to a few words that carry seeds for thoughts that I want to keep. Lynch, like Buffett, has the common-sense ability to say a lot with just a few words. Lynch coined some of the best known mantras of modern individual investing strategies:

The basic story remains simple and never-ending. Stocks aren't lottery tickets. There's a company attached to every share.

The key to making money in stocks is not to get scared out of them. You can find good reasons to scuttle your equities in every morning paper and on every broadcast of the nightly news.

If you're prepared to invest in a company, then you ought to be able to explain why in simple language that a fifth grader could understand, and quickly enough so the fifth grader won't get bored.

There's no shame in losing money on a stock. Everybody does it. What is shameful is to hold on to a stock, or worse, to buy more of it when the fundamentals are deteriorating.

In business, competition is never as healthy as total domination.

Your investor's edge is not something you get from Wall Street experts. It's something you already have. You can outperform the experts if you use your edge by investing in companies or industries you already understand.

I've found that when the market's going down and you buy funds wisely, at some point in the future you will be happy. You won't get there by reading 'Now is the time to buy.'

Owning stocks is like having children -- don't get involved with more than you can handle.

If you can't find any companies that you think are attractive, put your money in the bank (park it in the money market fund with your broker) until you discover some.

If you don't study any companies, you have the same success buying stocks as you do in a poker game if you bet without looking at your cards.

Time is on your side when you own shares of superior companies.

You have to keep your priorities straight if you plan to do well in stocks.

When you start to confuse Freddie Mac, Sallie Mae and Fannie Mae with members of your family, and you remember 2,000 stock symbols but forget the children's birthdays, there's a good chance you've become too wrapped up in your work.

If you're lucky enough to have been rewarded in life to the degree that I have, there comes a point at which you have to decide whether to become a slave to your net worth by devoting the rest of your life to increasing it or to let what you've accumulated begin to serve you.

The worst thing you can do is invest in companies you know nothing about. Unfortunately, buying stocks on ignorance is still a popular American pastime.

I'm always fully invested. It's a great feeling to be caught with your pants up.

Know what you own, and know why you own it.

In this business, if you're good, you're right six times out of ten. You're never going to be right nine times out of ten.

The person that turns over the most rocks wins the game. And that's always been my philosophy.

People who want to know how stocks fared on any given day ask, "Where did the Dow close?" I'm more interested in how many stocks went up versus how many went down. These so-called advance/decline numbers paint a more realistic picture.

It would be wonderful if we could avoid the setbacks with timely exits, but nobody has figured out how to predict them. (note: Lynch also said he didn't think anybody could predict a stock's price behavior out to one or two years.)

When people discover they are no good at baseball or hockey, they put away their bats and their skates and they take up amateur golf or stamp collecting or gardening. But when people discover they are no good at picking stocks, they are likely to continue to do it anyway.

That's not to say there's no such thing as an overvalued market, but there's no point worrying about it.

Investing in stocks is an art, not a science, and people who've been trained to rigidly quantify everything have a big disadvantage.

During the Gold Rush, most would-be miners lost money, but people who sold them picks, shovels, tents and blue-jeans (Levi Strauss) made a nice profit.

All you need for a lifetime of successful investing is a few big winners, and the pluses from those will overwhelm the minuses from the stocks that don't work out.

The Financial Brainwashing of America

When I set out to write this book for aspiring stock market investors, I realized the reason most people fail to save, is because they've been told to put the cart before the horse; they have been advised to save for retirement without considering a fact far more motivating: Savings is for improving your life now, not waiting until retirement.

The American public has been brainwashed with the wrong financial advice. Financial advisors tell people that, after having a few months salary in savings, that they should spend the rest of their lives putting money towards saving for retirement. I want you to consider something: **The people that have been telling you this, are the people who make money when you put your savings in their accounts!** Until you can achieve paycheck freedom, which is what I call an escape from daily financial worries, forget about putting your money in tax-free accounts that have huge penalties to keep you from using it. The 75% of our people living paycheck to paycheck don't have tax problems, they have income problems! Didn't you ever wonder why your IRA charges you a penalty, if you have to get to your own money – even if it's an emergency? The day you realize you can begin financial improvement right now, is the day you become motivated to change your financial habits.

Summary and Activities

- You know the major stock exchanges.

- You have a list of some popular and profitable stocks to explore.

- You understand what a stock dividend is, and the advantages of DRIP, dividend reinvestment plans.

- You have an online (free) calculator to see past performances of some great stocks.

- You understand P/E, P/S, Book Value.

- In Warren Buffett and Peter Lynch, you see how the most successful stock investors value common-sense, simple math, and their profound ideas about how 'simple' is always better.

- You understand that information overload is the enemy, and that sound investments are not made by 'hot' stocks and headline news stories.

Suggested Activities You Can Perform Now:

- Go online to a web browser and use some of the free calculators to see how some stocks have performed over the years. See: https://dqydj.com/stock-return-calculator-dividend-reinvestment-drip/

- Be sure to sample some of the many free online stock-charts; start getting familiar with these because you will come to rely on them to help you evaluate investments. See:
http://www.nasdaq.com/quotes/stock-charts.aspx
http://www.finance.yahoo.com
https://www.google.com/finance

- There are a number of free apps for apple and android devices; see your app store to download a couple of them. Most allow you to put in the symbols of popular stocks, so you can just 'click' to see the quotes during the day or after hours.

- Start to make your own list of stocks that interest you. The next chapter in this book is about selecting a broker and opening an account.

There are some great videos on YouTube.com featuring Warren Buffett & Peter Lynch. Search those names on YouTube.com and you can watch some remarkable videos. Even just listening to the audio while commuting is a great way to learn.

"Over the long term, the stock market news will be good. In the 20th century, the United States endured two world wars and other traumatic and expensive military conflicts; the Depression; a dozen or so recessions and financial panics; oil shocks; a flu epidemic; and the resignation of a disgraced president. Yet the Dow rose from 66 to 11,497." -Warren Buffett

Being in control of your finances is a great stress reliever.

Rich People stay rich by living like they are poor.

Poor People stay poor by living like they are rich.

SIMPLICITY IS THE ULTIMATE FORM OF SOPHISTICATION

Chapter 3
Opening Your Online Trading Account

The application process is very simple. The brokerage company will have you fill out a few forms to open the account, execute a (separate) margin agreement, and you will add an options agreement to your account (only if you wish to trade options). These applications will gather information on you to make sure you are credit worthy and that you have the experience and understanding to trade your account at the various levels they may approve.

When a person opens an account, they are assigned one of several option approval levels supposedly based on the option trader's knowledge and needs. If you plan to use Covered Call or Cash-Secured Put strategies (usually low risk strategies), you'll need to do this. If you are not sure, skip it; you can add it later with no problem. There is no fee involved; this is only an authorization level for individual traders. If you only want to trade stocks, you won't need an option agreement.

Experienced investors often qualify for all levels when they open the account, whether they intend to trade them initially or not; this keeps you from having to do more paperwork later, when you do wish to trade them. Anyone who is uncertain of their option approval level should read more about it (at OIC), or contact his or her broker to find out which level of option approval their account has.

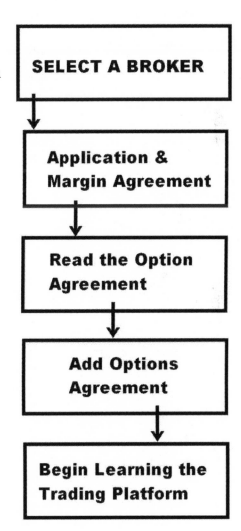

Normally, there are four option approval levels. There is no official standard of what strategies could be traded at which level. The categories described below are typical levels used by most trading companies. A level 4 can trade all four categories, a level 3 can also trade 1 and 2 but not 4, and so on.

Option Approval Levels	Strategies Approved
Level 1	Covered Call, Long Protective Puts
Level 2	Long call/put
Level 3	Spreads
Level 4	Uncovered or Naked

Beginners don't need the margin or options agreements. For more experienced investors: If you only want to buy CALLS and PUTS, and sell covered CALLS, a margin agreement is not required. If you want to place debit and credit spreads, you'll need to have the margin account. To trade more advanced strategies, the brokerage company needs to know you have the experience and financial resources to trade these higher levels.

You should read the technical brochure carefully – *Characteristics and Risks of Standardized Options* and make sure you understand the risky aspects of this type trading. You shouldn't have any problem understanding this brochure and the options agreement once you have read this book.

It is, by law, the brokers responsibility to gather this information on your financial resources and trading experience; most use a group of standardized questions on the applications.

You can read more about the LEVELS at:
 http://www.optionstrading.org/getting-started/trading-levels/
Understand which of these levels are suitable for you before you apply for the account so you can communicate clearly with your trading company.

The Functions of Your Online Broker

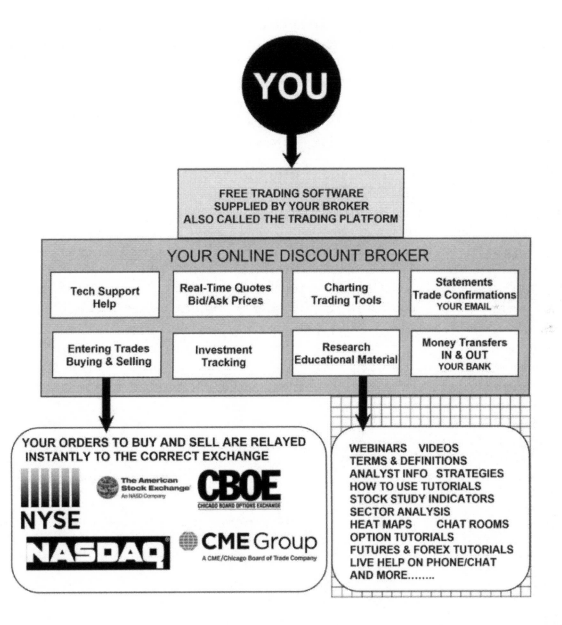

YOU

FREE TRADING SOFTWARE
SUPPLIED BY YOUR BROKER
ALSO CALLED THE TRADING PLATFORM

YOUR ONLINE DISCOUNT BROKER

Tech Support Help	Real-Time Quotes Bid/Ask Prices	Charting Trading Tools	Statements Trade Confirmations YOUR EMAIL
Entering Trades Buying & Selling	Investment Tracking	Research Educational Material	Money Transfers IN & OUT YOUR BANK

YOUR ORDERS TO BUY AND SELL ARE RELAYED INSTANTLY TO THE CORRECT EXCHANGE

NYSE

The American Stock Exchange
An NASD Company

CBOE
CHICAGO BOARD OPTIONS EXCHANGE

NASDAQ

CME Group
A CME/Chicago Board of Trade Company

WEBINARS   VIDEOS
TERMS & DEFINITIONS
ANALYST INFO   STRATEGIES
HOW TO USE TUTORIALS
STOCK STUDY INDICATORS
SECTOR ANALYSIS
HEAT MAPS   CHAT ROOMS
OPTION TUTORIALS
FUTURES & FOREX TUTORIALS
LIVE HELP ON PHONE/CHAT
AND MORE........

<u>Tech support:</u> It is quite normal if you are new to your broker - that you will have some questions on how to install and operate the software, a.k.a. "The trading platform." There are scores of training videos, articles, webinars, and written instructions either on line / in a manual to help you learn to operate the software. It is imperative that you open a practice session (paper trading account) so you can familiarize yourself with all operating aspects of the software and to learn about the services your broker offers. Some of the brokers have 'for fee' services; my advice it that until you gain a lot of experience, you do not sign up for any of those. You will find more than enough to explore and learn without buying additional services. You should try and find answers to your questions by viewing videos and reading instructions as much as you can. When you get stuck, phone your broker and they will get you going again. As a courtesy, it is the custom that you should be as quick and specific as you can when you phone them for help. Brokers usually have a text chat help service also.

<u>Real-Time Quotes Bid/Ask Prices:</u> One of the first things you'll do with your new online account is to build *watch lists*. You simply put in symbols of stocks you wish to follow and the software will give you the bid/ask prices, change for the day, the ability to pull up charts for each stock, ETF, or Index, and more.

<u>Charting-Trading Tools:</u> When you view charts, the horizontal axis will be time/dates and the vertical will display the prices. Begin using bar charts, which display the high, low for various (selected by you) intervals of time, like 1m, 5m,15m, 30m, 1h, 4h, 1d, 1w (minute, hour, day, week.) If you wish, you may learn more about technical indicators and charting in your software. There are a hundred or more indicators, but four or five of them are used most commonly: MACD, Bollinger Bands, Resistance-Support, Momentum, and so on. Your broker will have professionally made videos you can view free – on just about any subject.

<u>Statements and Trade Confirmations:</u> Your daily transaction summary, statements, and confirmation notifications are listed in the program and usually you will receive daily email notifications of your transactions. When you enter an order, you will get a 'fill' the moment a transaction occurs – and usually a sounder to alert you also. The 'fill' is the same as a confirmation and gives you time/date stamp, transactions, prices, and other information. Paper statements are normally sent at the end of each month, but you can get your account status and balance, and a record of your transactions anytime online.

<u>Entering Trades, Buying and Selling:</u> Follow the instructions to enter trades, you will enter the quantity, price, and the type of order you prefer to use. (Type of orders will be explained in a section in this book.) All trading software will allow you to enter an order, and then to check it again before you SEND it; this is to avoid mistakes.

<u>Investment Tracking:</u> There is a section in your trading platform that will always summarize your trades, current valuation of them, and list them in an easy to interpret format. This section is sometimes called *position summary* or another similar term.

<u>Research Educational Material:</u> Every online broker provides customers with many tools that include charts, news items, research material, and more to help you find the information you need. Anytime you need help, you can ask your broker to suggest videos so you can train to use the software's many valuable features. It will be time well spent. You can use your smartphone or other device to watch this material on your own convenient schedule. Also, most brokers provide chat rooms where customers can talk among themselves, and this is a way to find ideas and help.

<u>Money Transfers IN & OUT:</u> When you open your account, you may mail a check if you wish. Most commonly, monies are transferred in/out of your account by wire transfers (or an equivalent) directly from your bank. You can call account services of your broker and they can help you set this up and answer your questions. Be aware, some banks and/or brokers charge varying rates for these services. Ask your broker for suggestions, if you need help in finding the best way for your particular needs. Often, banks have ridiculous fees to make these transfers, so be sure and ask 'how much' before you authorize the transfer.

Choosing a Broker

Online brokers typically charge from $4.95 to $12.95 per transaction (regardless of the number of shares you are trading of a stock.) To be clear: Whether you buy one share or a thousand shares, each transaction will be charged this flat fee. There is one transaction for each security (stock); you can't combine stocks into one order. Often brokers will offer a number of free trades to new accounts, so ask about that when you call.

While brokers who charge $9.95 for a trade are charging almost double the $4.95 rate, it is better to use a broker that has good software, technical service, and is a good fit for you –

rather than trying to save a few dollars on stock commissions. You might save $5, but wind up with software you don't particularly like; this is not advisable. *In the long run a few dollars more in commissions here and there should not be a deal-breaker if you get the broker you like.* Where you might pay $9.95 for a trade, you are still getting a good deal since full-service fees easily range from $25 and up.

Here's a partial list of some brokers you may wish to consider; go to their web sites and take a look at their trading platform (most will provide you samples or at least a video).

TD Ameritrade: ThinkOrSwim   ETrade
Fidelity   OptionHouse
Scott Trade   TradeKing
Charles Schwab

Often brokers will have more than one version of software. For example: a simple version for just buying and selling stocks; this version uses the simplest of screen interfaces and is very easy to use. Secondly, most experienced traders will opt for the version (still absolutely free) that has more features. This advanced version offers more flexibility and services. Most companies allow you to use them interchangeably – and you can switch back and forth effortlessly. Ask about this when you phone them.

The Importance of the Trade Simulation Mode

Sometimes, starting off with the more complicated trading software can be off-putting to beginners and they opt for the simpler version until they gain some confidence. Remember that your broker will have a trade simulation mode where you can learn to use the software without having to use real money. Your mistakes there won't cost you anything; this is a valuable service to learn to use the software, so go for it, explore and learn. This can be quite fun to trade paper money until you get the hang of things.

The experience of using a broker's software can vary widely, so you might wish to compare two or three before you decide. The brokers understand this; they help new customers every day. Ask questions, and see how user friendly your new broker will be!

The importance of learning to use the convenience and power of the trading software furnished to you by your broker cannot be overemphasized. Not too long ago, trading 'paper money' accounts, merely kept a list of trades and P/L (profit/loss). Now, you must learn to think of your trading software as your control center of trading and research. Being able to use your software is key to your success; it has powerful features and it will serve you well to spend the time to learn to use it. Your broker has free videos to make learning easy. Viewing several *short* videos works much better than watching hour-long videos – and this avoids information overload. As you are trading it is important to have confidence in your ability to find and use information. Use the trade simulation mode of your broker like a pilot would use a flight simulator. Think of it as a valuable and accurate trading tool and hone your skills with it so you can remain focused on your trading and not have half your attention diluted by not learning to use your software seamlessly. It's actually quite fun to trade in 'paper money' mode. It's a great way to test some ideas and gain confidence and experience without any of the risks.

Don't spend money you don't have...

To Buy things you don't need...

For People you don't like.

-Will Rogers

If you want to feel rich, just count the things you have that money can't buy.

Most Popular Stocks by Demographics

:

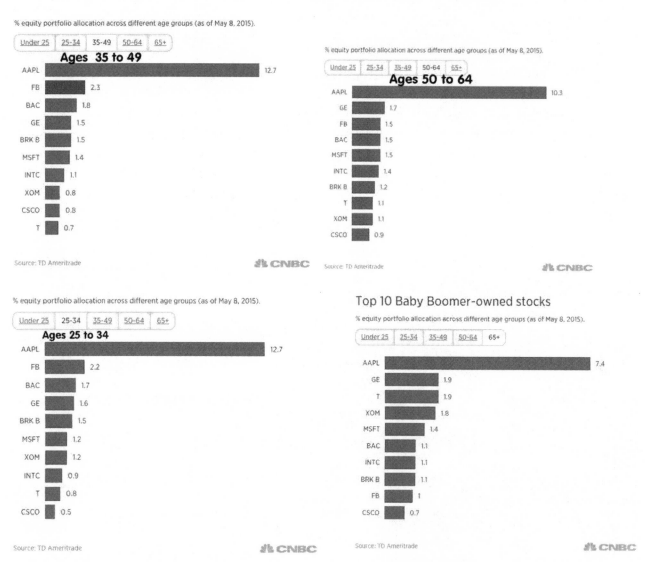

% equity portfolio allocation across different age groups (as of May 8, 2015).

| Under 25 | 25-34 | 35-49 | 50-64 | 65+ |

Ages 35 to 49

Stock	Value
AAPL	12.7
FB	2.3
BAC	1.8
GE	1.5
BRK B	1.5
MSFT	1.4
INTC	1.1
XOM	0.8
CSCO	0.8
T	0.7

Source: TD Ameritrade

% equity portfolio allocation across different age groups (as of May 8, 2015).

| Under 25 | 25-34 | 35-49 | 50-64 | 65+ |

Ages 50 to 64

Stock	Value
AAPL	10.3
GE	1.7
FB	1.5
BAC	1.5
MSFT	1.5
INTC	1.4
BRK B	1.2
T	1.1
XOM	1.1
CSCO	0.9

Source: TD Ameritrade

% equity portfolio allocation across different age groups (as of May 8, 2015).

| Under 25 | 25-34 | 35-49 | 50-64 | 65+ |

Ages 25 to 34

Stock	Value
AAPL	12.7
FB	2.2
BAC	1.7
GE	1.6
BRK B	1.5
MSFT	1.2
XOM	1.2
INTC	0.9
T	0.8
CSCO	0.5

Source: TD Ameritrade

Top 10 Baby Boomer-owned stocks

% equity portfolio allocation across different age groups (as of May 8, 2015).

| Under 25 | 25-34 | 35-49 | 50-64 | 65+ |

Stock	Value
AAPL	7.4
GE	1.9
T	1.9
XOM	1.8
MSFT	1.4
BAC	1.1
INTC	1.1
BRK B	1.1
FB	1
CSCO	0.7

Source: TD Ameritrade

% of portfolios as of May 8, 2015

Chapter 4
Buy Stocks Without a Brokerage Account

What you are about to read may be one of the best kept secrets of personal finance. *It really isn't a secret at all, it's just one of those things that you never hear about because nobody gets paid to tell you about it.* It is the most inexpensive and easy way for you to own stock, and then buy more and more stock at zero commissions. It's the DRIP that has already been discussed partially – The **D**ividend **ReI**nvestment **P**lan

Usually, the easiest way to set up a DRIP is:
1)   First, if you have a brokerage account, ask your broker if they can do it for you. Be sure and ask what, if anything, they will charge for this service. Some brokers can do it free, others charge for it. Either way, the charges are usually small.

2)   Whether you have a brokerage account or not, you can call the company or email their *shareholder services* department and ask for information about their dividend reinvestment plan. It is normal that you must have at least one share of a company to participate. Some companies may refer you to a third party to set up your DRIP, and this means you must pay a one-time fee. You can also Google for information on a company's *shareholder services* or DRIP. Accounts can usually be set up for minors with a social security number.

3)   Another advantage that often comes with joining a DRIP is the ability to buy additional shares of stock at no commission. For example, some companies allow you to buy up to $250,000 per year with no commissions to pay. Be sure to ask shareholder services for the specifics about this choice. Some of these DRIPs are very generous that way.

4)   You should know that you have the choice to set up individual accounts or a joint account. JTWROS (Joint Tenants With Right of Survivorship)

Here's a few Q&A's that may give you some ideas and information about DRIPs:

Question: *What if I don't have a brokerage account, is there an easy and inexpensive way I can start buying stock with just a little money?*
Answer: You might consider one of the dividend paying stocks mentioned in this book, or find them on your own. Once you pick a stock, Google the company's name with the term *shareholder services.*   For example Google this term: *Home Depot shareholder services* or *Coca Cola shareholders services. Tell them you want info on the DRIP, dividend reinvestment plan. If one company can't help you, try another; they are not all the same.*

Note: It is very common for companies to use a third-party registered broker (Computershare for example) to help you get setup with a DRIP. The minimum amount required to start can vary, as does the minimum amount for monthly contributions. These fees are normally quite reasonable. After you get setup, you can buy additional stock by the month, weekly check, autobank withdrawal, or random contributions. Do not hesitate to ask the shareholder services your questions. Make sure you understand the terms before you participate.

Question: *What if I want to set up and account in a DRIP for a child or grandchild?*
Answer: It's very easy and it's done all the time. Just tell shareholder services what you want to do and they will help you. When setting up accounts for minors, they will need a social security number.

Question: *How do I find out what dividends stocks pay? Do all stocks pay dividends?*
Answer: Ask your broker, look it up online, or ask shareholder services. No, all stocks do not pay dividends. When dividends are paid, your DRIP will automatically buy additional shares with those funds. If the funds are less than the price of one share, partial shares will be purchased based on the current trading value of the stock. There are no charges for these dividends to make these purchases. By opening a DRIP and allowing dividends to buy more shares, you will accumulate more shares over time than if you did not use this method. The additional shares you buy will also be paying you dividends – compounding growth of your account balance.

Question: I've never opened a DRIP before, so I'm not sure what I should say or ask. What advice do you offer?

Answer: No worries. Most people who contact a company's shareholder services are in the same boat as you. They know how to handle your requests and generally they are very helpful and knowledgeable people.

Remember: If you Google or phone a company wanting information about a Dividend Reinvestment Plan, ask (or search) for: *shareholder services*

Example: Google for: Coca Cola shareholder services

They can give you all the information you need and will help you set up an account. You set up an account with each stock (company) that you call. There is no limit on how many DRIPs you can set up for you and/or your children (minors).

Invest in yourself

Formal education will make you a living; self-education will make you a fortune.
--Jim Rohn

How many millionaires do you know who have become wealthy by investing in savings accounts? I rest my case.   --Robert G. Allen

You must gain control over your money or the lack of it will forever control you.
--Dave Ramsey

It's not how much money you make, but how much money you keep, how hard it works for you, and how many generations you keep it for.   --Robert Kiyosaki

Twenty years from now you will be more disappointed by the things that you didn't do than by the ones you did do. --Mark Twain

When buying shares, ask yourself, would you buy the whole company? --Rene Rivkin

Chapter 5
Exchange Traded Funds - ETF

ETFs are not complicated. they are essentially a basket of investments that trade exactly like stocks and can have the diversity of a mutual fund. If you are not familiar, a mutual fund allows you to buy shares of a basket of stocks so you spread the risk to many stocks instead of one.

The great thing about ETFs is that they trade just like stocks, you can buy and sell them at will during regular market hours. ETFs allow you to pursue very specific investment goals and still maintain diversity. For example, the S&P 500 Index tracks 500 stocks and is representative of overall stock market investment results. If you want an investment that will give you the same return as owning those 500 stocks, then you can buy an ETF that is the equivalent. One popular fund that does this is called "The Spyder", symbol: SPY. Since inception in 1993, it has returned about 9% per year.

Fund Performance

SPDR	MONTH END As of 10/31/2016
1 Month	-1.82%
QTD	-1.82%
YTD	5.74%
1 Year	4.41%
3 Year	8.73%
5 Year	13.41%
10 Year	6.60%
Inception	8.90%

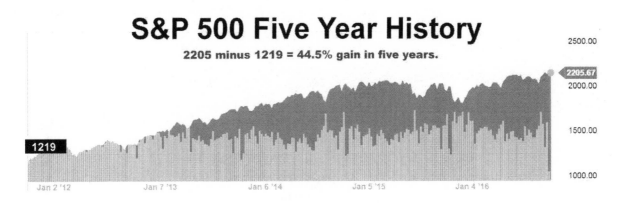

S&P 500 Five Year History
2205 minus 1219 = 44.5% gain in five years.

The flexibility and sector targeting that ETFs offer is amazing. You may have heard that many investors think it wise to have a part of their nest egg in gold. One way to accomplish that is to buy a gold Exchange Traded Fund; there are over a dozen different ones.

There are ETFs available in virtually any sector, like these and more:

- High tech

- Growth Stocks

- Any major index

- Utility

- Dividend stocks real estate

- Commodities

- Foreign Currency

- Bonds

- Energy

- Oil

- Foreign Stocks Pharmaceuticals

You should know that you get charts and stats on ETFs just like you can on stocks. The market capitalization of ETFs can be important; some funds are so small that liquidity is limited.

There are firms that specialize in ETF evaluations and analysis and can offer information and assistance on ETF choices. See: morningstar.com and explore the site for a myriad of articles and information about ETFs. They offer premium (pay) services and plenty of free information. It's a great site to learn more and they discuss the use of ETFs in trading.

Chapter 6
Stock Trading Terms

Almost every business has its own jargon and stock trading is no different. If you have zero experience in stock trading, getting acquainted with commonly used terms is a bit like entering a foreign culture and having to learn the language. You will need to know the language of trading and the effort you make will payoff for you the rest of your life. The terms presented here are the most common and often used. Many of the terms you see all the time, others you will rarely see. Better to look them up as you need them, instead of trying to learn them all. These are a few that are very common:

Liquidity, Volume, and OI (Open Interests): How quickly and easily one may find buyers and sellers of a stock is a matter of its *liquidity*. If relatively few people trade a stock, the stock probably has a very small *market capitalization*. You should normally stay away from these securities; this is because when a stock trades with *high volume*, there are lots of buyers and sellers for it – and it is easy and *efficient* to get in and out of.

Bid/Ask: The Bid price of a stock, called "the bid", is the price someone is willing to pay for the stock. The Ask price, called "the ask" is the price for which someone is willing to sell the stock. Normally on a liquid stock with good daily trading volume the bid/ask has a narrow *gap*. For example: Shares of Wells-Fargo (WFC) might be quoted at: "55.12/55.13"; there is a $0.01 or one-cent gap in the bid/ask. If the bid/ask displays a wide gap, it probably means a stock is not trading efficiently. In such cases, one could buy a stock and then sell it immediately and lose money. For example: If the bid/ask was quoted as: "34.75/35.15", a gap of $0.40. You will notice that normal stocks with good *market cap* and *trading volume* have narrow *gaps*. When you start using your trading software, you will see quotes as 'bid/ask' and the 'last', meaning *last trade price*. If the bid/ask is *away* from the last trade; it could mean the stock hasn't traded recently (or maybe you are looking after trading hours).

EPS Earnings Per Share: Most companies post their earnings reports each quarter. Usually, EPS are compared to the same quarter a year ago. This is because merely comparing to last quarter does not take into account the seasonality of a business. For example: Many retailers do a great percentage of their business in the fourth quarter during the holiday shopping.

Volatility: This is the degree of variation over a period of time. Generally speaking, when a stock's price makes frequent and/or larger changes; its volatility increases. Realize that a stock's volatility does not measure the direction of price changes, merely their dispersion. The volatility of a stock is reflected in its *beta*; the higher the beta, the more volatile is the stock's price. This term, volatility, is also used when describing the market in general.

BETA is the measure of volatility, or systematic risk, of a security or portfolio in comparison to the market as a whole.

VIX is the ticker symbol for the Chicago Board Options Exchange (CBOE) Volatility Index, which shows the market's expectation of 30-day volatility. It is constructed using the implied volatilities of a wide range of S&P 500 index options. This volatility is meant to be forward looking, is calculated from market derivatives on stocks, and is a widely used measure of market risk, often referred to as the "investor fear gauge." The VIX (symbol) gauges the S&P 500, which allows for a view of investors' expectations on future market volatility. VIX values greater than 30 are generally associated with a large amount of volatility as a result of investor fear or uncertainty, while values below 20 generally correspond to less stressful, even complacent, times in the markets.

It is good that you understand what beta of a stock is, and what general market volatility (as measured by VIX) is – but when you are studying an individual stock, there are more practical ways of understanding how volatile your stock may be. It is wise to put a stock into your watch list; by seeing its price over time (weeks and months), you will come to know its price behavior, how much the price normally varies in a day's trading, its price history, and the types of news and greater market moves that affect its price. You also use the historical price chart of a stock to determine many of these things.

Guidance, Estimated Earnings: When companies issue *guidance*; this means they may portend how the company may perform in the future. They might raise or lower their own estimated earnings projections or "change guidance" – and this can have immediately effects on a stock's price. Guidance is information a company provides as an indication or estimate of its future earnings. It is an "expected results" issued from a company to shareholders and market watchers as to how it envisions a future period of time. Such guidance typically includes revenue estimates, along with earnings, margins and capital spending estimates; it is also known as *earnings guidance*. While companies are not required to provide earnings guidance, it is a common practice. Most companies provide earnings guidance during specific financial releases and discussions. It is commonly provided with a company's quarterly earnings report and comments. Companies may also provide guidance with specific market transactions or during analyst meetings and conference calls.

Types of Orders

An *order* is a direction to your broker to buy or sell. A trader is said to *issue* an order. It is the same as using your software to *send* an order. Always double check orders before you send them, it is your responsibility to enter correct orders. If you are not sure you are entering an order correctly, then call your broker and ask for some help. Never make assumptions. This is another advantage of practicing with your paper-trading account; making mistakes there doesn't cost you money. It is also your responsibility to know the type of order you are issuing.

Market Orders: A *market (mkt) order* is when you buy or sell at the prevailing price quote of a stock. For example when your stock is quoted bid/ask at: 42.55/42.56 When you enter a *market order to buy*, the trade will be executed at 42.56, the *ask* price. When you enter a *market order to sell*, the trade will be executed at 42.55, the *bid* price. A market order does not contain a specific price but will accept whatever ask/offer price is *at the market*. Market orders are executed, during market hours, instantly.

Limit Orders: A *limit order* is when you issue an order with a specific price; if that price is not available, the order stands until it can be executed. A limit order may or may not be executed. You are allowed to change the price in a limit order, to cancel it, or to cancel it and replace it with another type of order or a different price – it takes only a few seconds to do this. When there is a significant gap in the bid/ask gap, it can be advisable to issue a limit order. Also in a *fast market* (a market when prices are changing rapidly), one can use a limit order so you are not subject to a fast price change and get filled at an undesirable price. Limit orders remain unfilled, until a buyer or seller at its price are trading.

Another use for limit orders is when you feel your price might be met during the trading day; your price may be above or below the current quote, but you want to put the order up with the hope that it will be filled. If you forget about the order, you are still responsible for it, so pay attention at all times. Orders may be cancelled or changed anytime during the trading day. To review all this, ask your broker to point you to a video on 'types of orders.'

Day and GTC orders: Your orders are by default *day* orders; this means they are good for the current trading session (the day's trading hours) and they will not carry forward to the next session and they will be cancelled at the end of day's trading. GTC or good-till-cancelled orders remain as the name suggests good until you cancel them. Brokers will carry a GTC order until you cancel it, which is your responsibility.

To illustrate how GTC orders work: Say you know beyond any doubt you wish to buy shares of XYZ stock at a price of $37.41 cents. You may enter a limit order of 'buy at $37.41 GTC". Conversely, if you own XYZ shares and you wish to sell them when the stock reaches a price of $50.25, you enter a limit order to sell at $50.25 GTC. Always assume your GTC orders remain in effect until you actively cancel them or until they are filled. If you are not clear on how to know if you are entering an order as either limit or market, ask your broker for instructions- never assume. If a mistake is made, it is on you, not your broker.

Stop-Limit Order: A stop-limit order will be executed at a specified price (or better) after a given stop price has been reached. Once the stop price is reached, the stop-limit order becomes a *limit* order to buy (or sell) at the limit price or better. This order may or may not be filled.

A Stop Order: Sometimes called *stop-loss order*, is an order to buy or sell a stock once the price of the stock reaches a specified price, known as the *stop price*. When the stop price is reached, a stop order becomes a *market order*. A buy–stop order is entered at a stop price above the current *market* price. Investors generally use a buy stop order to limit a loss or to protect a profit on a stock that they have sold short. A sell–stop order is entered at a stop price below the current market price. Investors generally use a sell–stop order to limit a loss or to protect a profit on a stock that they own. This stop-loss order is the order you use when you want to make sure you limit your losses and you may not be watching the stock prices during trading hours.

When the stop price is reached, and the stop order becomes a *market* order, this means the trade will definitely be executed, but not necessarily at or near the stop price, particularly when the order is placed into a fast-moving market, or if there is insufficient liquidity available relative to the size of the order. Stop orders are generally not used by beginners; study up on them if you plan to use one. They can be tricky.

OCO: There are other kinds of orders for special circumstances. An **OCO order** is One Order Cancels the Other. you can put in two orders simultaneously and the first one to trigger will cancel the other. These are not often used by beginners.

Slippage: Slippage occurs when a trade is executed at a different price than what was expected. The amounts are usually very small, but slippage can be avoided by not using market orders when they are not necessary. You should remember, if you need to close or open a trade fast, a *market* order might be necessary –otherwise, the *limit* order is the preferred order type. Periods of volatility, large orders and market orders can all lead to slippage. *Liquid* stocks are frequently traded, and their supply and demand will usually keep their price stable. But *illiquid* stocks are thinly traded, and one big order can cause significant slippage. The *daily volume*, usually just called *volume* (vol), statistic will tell you how many shares have been traded on a trading day.

Please note that the default type of order term, is the *day order;* day orders, if not executed, expire at the end of that day's trading. GTC, good-till-cancelled, orders are reentered automatically until you cancel them. After trading and gaining experience, these details will become almost second-nature to you. *If you have any doubt about what type or term of any of your orders, call your broker and they will help you verify the details of your order before you send it.* This is another opportunity to use your paper-money account for practice: Enter an order, change it to another price, then change it from the (default) day order to a GTC order. Practicing these tasks before you need them is a good idea.

The GTC order uses: Here's an example of how you could use a GTC order: Suppose XYZ stock is currently trading at 43.56 per share, and you intend to buy shares if the stock goes down to 40.00 per share. You might issue a buy-GTC order at 40.00. When the stock trades at your price, you order will be executed. *Technically, an order has to pass through your trade for you to be guaranteed a fill; for example if XYZ trades at 39.99, you would certainly be filled.* If it only trades 40.00, you may or may not be filled depending on the orders that were ahead of you. Orders are traded in the order they are entered. It is actually not unusual for a stock to be traded at the price of your order, and you *not* get filled; it has to trade *through* your price, before you are entitled to get filled.

Annualized Return

The percentage of annualized return is very important; this is the term that allows you to compare 'apples-to-apples', the common denominator of stock performance, the unit of measurement that is used for universal comparison. This is like the miles-per-hour (or kilometers per hour) measurement on an automobiles speedometer. If a stock price moves up 120% in ten years, the average annualized return is 12%. There are some qualifications to an annualized return. For example, if a stock pays dividends, one would usually compute *the annualized return with dividends reinvested*, to find an exact return.

The Rule of 72 and the Magic of Compound Interest

This rule is used to explain what is often called *the magic of compound interest*. This is a shortcut to calculate returns in simple language and it happens to be very accurate. Here is the rule of 72 stated simply in a couple of ways:

To compute how many years it takes your money to double, divide the annualized return into 72.

Example: If you get an annualize return of 8%, it will take 9 years for your money to double.
72 divided by 8% = 9 years

To compute the annualized (%) return needed to double your money, divide 72 by the number of years.

Example:
If you wish to double your money in 12 years, you will need to make an annual return of 6%.
72 divided by 12 years = 6%

Here's another sample problem: Suppose you have $10,000 invested in a CD (Certificate of Deposit) at your bank and it pays 3.5% compounded annually. How long will it take to double your money?

Answer: 72 divided by 3.5% = 21.4 years

Suppose you invest in a stock that gets an annualized return of 8.9% (the approximate amount of return for the S&P 500 stock index since inception.) How many years would it take to double the same $10,000?

Answer: 72 divided by 8.9% = 8.08 year to double your money.

Question: Suppose a credit card issuer charges 18% interest per year. How long would it take for them to double their money?
Answer: 72 divided by 18% = 4.16 years.

This is why you should consider paying off credit cards and not be so eager to invest your money into a bank CD!

\$2500 per year at age 5 and 6			\$2500 per year ages 5 to 18		
Return at 10% per Year			Return at 10% per year		
Age	Invested	End of year	Age	Invested	End of year
5	\$2,500.00	\$2,750.00	5	\$2,500.00	\$2,750.00
6	\$2,500.00	\$5,775.00	6	\$2,500.00	\$5,775.00
7		\$6,352.50	7	\$2,500.00	\$9,102.50
8		\$6,987.75	8	\$2,500.00	\$12,762.75
9		\$7,686.53	9	\$2,500.00	\$16,789.03
10		\$8,455.18	10	\$2,500.00	\$21,217.93
11		\$9,300.70	11	\$2,500.00	\$26,089.72
12		\$10,230.76	12	\$2,500.00	\$31,448.69
13		\$11,253.84	13	\$2,500.00	\$37,343.56
14		\$12,379.23	14	\$2,500.00	\$43,827.92
15		\$13,617.15	15	\$2,500.00	\$50,960.71
16		\$14,978.86	16	\$2,500.00	\$58,806.78
17		\$16,476.75	17	\$2,500.00	\$67,437.46
18		\$18,124.42	18	\$2,500.00	\$76,931.20
19		\$19,936.87	19	0	\$84,624.32
20		\$21,930.55	20	0	\$93,086.76
25		\$35,319.37	25	0	\$149,917.15
30		\$56,882.21	30	0	\$241,443.07
35		\$91,609.36	35	0	\$388,846.49
40		\$147,537.79	40	0	\$626,241.15
45		\$237,611.09	45	0	\$1,008,567.64
50		\$382,675.04	50	0	\$1,624,308.27
55		\$616,301.98	55	0	\$2,615,964.71
60		\$992,560.50	60	0	\$4,213,037.33
61		\$1,091,816.55	61	0	\$4,634,341.06
62		\$1,200,998.20	62	0	\$5,097,775.17
63		\$1,321,098.02	63	0	\$5,607,552.69
64		\$1,453,207.83	64	0	\$6,168,307.96
65		\$1,598,528.61	65	0	\$6,785,138.75

Chapter 7
How to Explore and Learn More About Specific Stocks

The charts, comments, and information in this chapter are not intended as trading recommendations; they are here to illustrate some of the aspects of stock evaluations that may or may not be suitable for your particular investment goals. You should use the interactive websites flagged here or your broker's software and get up-to-date stats on these and other stocks. The more you practice, the more you'll understand.

Apple

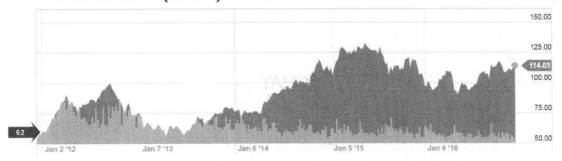

This chart and accompanying data is from Yahoo Financial on the Web at finance.yahoo.com

52-Week Range: 89.47 – 118.69

Average Daily Vol: 37,210,728

Market Cap: $608.29 Billion

Beta: 1.42

PE Ratio: 13.73

EPS: $8.31

Dividend & Yield: 2.28 (2.09%)

fy Target Est: 130.96

The "fy Target Est" is an average of 43 market analyst who cover Apple, Inc. The stock has an overall "buy" rating, where "strong buy" is the most positive category. Note the value of all outstanding shares of common stock is about $608 billion. At the time of these stats (DEC of 2016) the S&P 500 average P/E was 24.22.

As of DEC 2016, the EPS projections for the 4th Quarter are $3.22 per share. In the fall of calendar 2017, the new iPhone is expected to be a best-seller and will have wireless charging and other innovations which some think will mean strong sales.

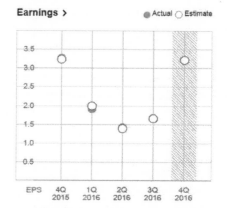

Similar type companies are: MSFT, HP, Acer, and Dell. It is normal when comparing the stats of companies to compare to similar companies. You can practice now if you go to finance.yahoo.com and look up AAPL competitors.

Often headline news stories might feature a company's newest innovations. For example new additions to AAPL's Apple TV or music services. As an investor, you must learn to measure the importance of these developments by asking questions such as, "How much of AAPL's total revenue is due to music and its video services, when compared to new product innovations and hardware sales?" This will enable you to better judge the impact of each segment of its business.

The longer you follow the news of stocks you own and those that you have an interest in purchasing, the more you know. Usually "hot stock tips" and stories are not the sorts of news that should heavily influence your long-term investments. Penny stocks, and start-ups are not where your money should be no matter how tempting it may sound; these stocks are unproven and not yet worthy of your hard earned dollars. The same is generally true for IPOs. IPO are new stocks whose shares are being offered for the first time (Initial Public Offerings.)

Remember that PE ratios are paramount in a stock's evaluation. It is not the cost of a share of stock, but the PE that tells you whether a stock might be *expensive* or *cheap*. For example a $10 stock with $1 earnings is generally a better value than an $80 stock with $5 earnings per share. Some companies decide to keep the cost per share high and some prefer to keep it low (instead of *splitting* the stock), but it's earnings-per-share that is a reliable indicator of the relative value of the stock. Various segments of the market carry different PE ranges, so you compare a stock's value to *similar* companies.

Most books that introduce personal investors to the stock market, use examples of "XYZ" stock, fictitious shares in the examples to teach so-called stock market theory. In preparing this book, I've taken a different path, not to steer the reader to any particular stock, but I do think it matters greatly that the reader can learn in a more realistic setting that better emulates the decisions that investors face. I've chosen stocks that are, for the most part, household names. Of course the data has changed accordingly since the publication date.

Disney

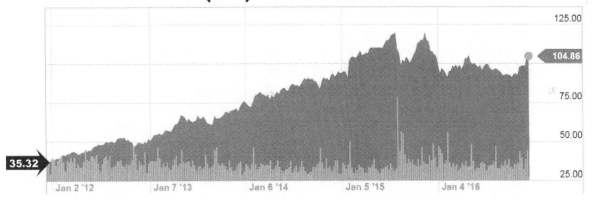

DISNEY (DIS) FIVE YEAR RETURN 196%

This chart and accompanying data is from Yahoo Financial on the Web at finance.yahoo.com

52-Week Range: 86.25 – 114.75

Average Daily Vol: 8,215,723

Market Cap: $166.88 Billion

Beta: 1.46

PE Ratio: 18.30

EPS: $5.73

Dividend & Yield: 1.56 (1.55%)

fy Target Est: 106.68

The Walt Disney Company, commonly known as Disney, is an American diversified multinational mass media and entertainment conglomerate headquartered at the Walt Disney Studios in Burbank, California. It is the world's second largest media conglomerate in terms of revenue, after Comcast. Disney was founded on October 16, 1923, by brothers Walt Disney and Roy O. Disney as the Disney Brothers Cartoon Studio, and established itself as a leader in the American animation industry before diversifying into live-action film production, television, and theme parks. The company also operated under the names The Walt Disney Studio then Walt Disney Productions. Taking on its current name in 1986, it expanded its existing operations and also started divisions focused upon theater, radio, music, publishing, and online media.

In addition, Disney has since created corporate divisions in order to market more mature content than is typically associated with its flagship family-oriented brands. The company is best known for the products of its film studio, Walt Disney Studios, which is today one of the largest and best-known studios in American cinema. Disney's other three main divisions are Walt Disney Parks and Resorts, Disney Media Networks, and Disney Consumer Products and Interactive Media. Disney also owns and operates the ABC broadcast television network; cable television networks such as Disney Channel, ESPN, A+E Networks, and Freeform; publishing, merchandising, music, and theatre divisions; and owns and licenses 14 theme parks around the world. The company has been a component of the Dow Jones Industrial Average since May 6, 1991. Mickey Mouse, an early and well-known cartoon creation of the company, is a primary symbol and mascot for Disney.

In any company as diverse as Disney, there will be various divisions up and down at any given time. One of the reasons for featuring DIS here, is that it offers individual investors a way to buy shares directly from the company, and the option of a DRIP (dividend reinvestment plan). Some parents use stocks like Disney and its DRIP, to help introduce their children to investment concepts. If you want to know more about how this works, see this link on the web: http://shareholder.broadridge.com/disneyinvestor You can read about it or phone them for more details – and they will help you set it up; it is a fairly simple process and it doesn't take much money at all to do it.

Cracker Barrel Old Country Store, Inc. (CBRL)

Cracker Barrel Old Country Store, Inc. develops and operates the Cracker Barrel Old Country Store concept in the United States. The company's Cracker Barrel stores consist of a restaurant with a gift shop. Its restaurants serve breakfast, lunch, and dinner. The company's gift shops offer various decorative and functional items, such as rocking chairs, holiday and seasonal gifts, toys, apparels, music CDs, cookware, a book-on-audio sale-and-exchange program, and various other gift items, as well as candies, preserves, pies, cornbread mixes, coffee, syrups, pancake mixes, and other food items. As of November 22, 2016, it operated 641 Cracker Barrel stores in 43 states. Cracker Barrel Old Country Store, Inc. was founded in 1969 and is headquartered in Lebanon, Tennessee. It has about 73,000 employees.

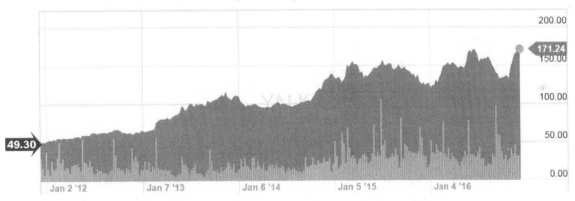

This chart and accompanying datra is from Yahoo Financial on the web at finance.yahoo.com

52-Week Range: 118.01- 172.89

Average Daily Vol: 398,784

Market Cap: $4.12 Billion

Beta: 0.45

PE Ratio: 20.96

EPS: $8.17

Dividend & Yield: 4.60 (2.69%)

You can see payments of CBRL dividends (below table). This book does not make investment recommendations, however you may check out this link: http://investor.cbrlgroup.com/faq.cfm and see some FAQ's (frequently asked questions) as an example of how easy it is to enroll/participant in Dividend Reinvestment Plans, and how to buy shares of a company directly. Sometimes there is a small fee through a brokerage company to set up the plan, but then buying shares and DRIP services are provided at no fees. Initial investments can be as low as $25 in many of these type plans – and whatever money you put in, will buy partial shares (so don't let the price of a company's stock deter you from looking into this.)

Ex-Div. Date	Amount	Type	Yield (annualized)		Declared	Ex-Date	Amount
1/11/2017	$1.15	Quarter	2.70%				
10/12/2016	$1.15	Quarter	3.50%		22-Nov-16	11-Jan-17	1.15
7/13/2016	$1.15	Quarter	3%		Total		1.15
4/13/2016	$1.10	Quarter	2.90%		26-Sep-16	12-Oct-16	1.15
1/13/2016	$1.10	Quarter	3.60%		1-Jun-16	13-Jul-16	3.25
10/14/2015	$1.10	Quarter	3.20%		1-Jun-16	13-Jul-16	1.15
7/15/2015	$3.00	Special	2%		29-Feb-16	13-Apr-16	1.1
7/15/2015	$1.10	Quarter	2.90%		9-Dec-15	13-Jan-16	1.1
4/15/2015	$1.00	Quarter	2.80%		Total		7.75
1/14/2015	$1.00	Quarter	3%		28-Sep-15	14-Oct-15	1.1
10/15/2014	$1.00	Quarter	3.70%		2-Jun-15	15-Jul-15	3
4/15/2014	$0.75	Quarter	3.20%		2-Jun-15	15-Jul-15	1.1
1/15/2014	$0.75	Quarter	2.90%		27-Feb-15	15-Apr-15	1
10/16/2013	$0.75	Quarter	2.90%		5-Dec-14	14-Jan-15	1
7/17/2013	$0.75	Quarter	3%		Total		7.2
4/17/2013	$0.50	Quarter	2.50%		3-Oct-14	15-Oct-14	1
1/16/2013	$0.50	Quarter	3.10%		28-Apr-14	16-Jul-14	1
10/17/2012	$0.50	Quarter	3%		28-Feb-14	15-Apr-14	0.75
7/18/2012	$0.40	Quarter	2.50%		6-Dec-13	15-Jan-14	0.75
4/18/2012	$0.25	Quarter	1.80%				
1/18/2012	$0.25	Quarter	0.60%				
10/19/2011	$0.25	Quarter	0.60%				
7/13/2011	$0.22	Quarter	0.50%				

Johnson & Johnson (JNJ)

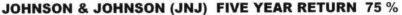

JOHNSON & JOHNSON (JNJ) FIVE YEAR RETURN 75 %

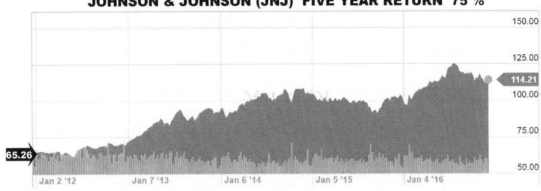

This chart and accompanying data is from Yahoo Financial on the Web at finance.yahoo.com

52-Week Range: 94.28 – 114.67

Average Daily Vol: 7.219 Million

Market Cap: $310.74 Billion

Beta: 0.64

PE Ratio: 20.05

EPS: $5.7

Dividend & Yield: 3.2 (2.85%)

Johnson & Johnson, together with its subsidiaries, researches and develops, manufactures, and sells various products in the health care field worldwide. It operates through three segments: Consumer, Pharmaceutical, and Medical Devices. The Consumer segment offers baby care products under the JOHNSONS brand name; oral care products under the LISTERINE brand name; skin care products under the AVEENO, CLEAN & CLEAR, DABAO, JOHNSONS Adult, LE PETITE MARSEILLAIS, LUBRIDERM, NEUTROGENA, and brand names; womens health products, such as sanitary pads under the STAYFREE and CAREFREE, and o.b. tampon brand names; wound care products, including adhesive bandages under the BAND-AID brand name and first aid products under the NEOSPORIN brand name. This segment also provides over-the-counter medicines, including acetaminophen products under the TYLENOL brand name; cold, flu, and allergy products under the SUDAFED brand name; allergy products under the BENADRYL and ZYRTEC brand names; ibuprofen products under the

MOTRIN IB brand name; and heartburn products under the PEPCID brand name. The Pharmaceutical segment provides various products in the areas of immunology, infectious diseases and vaccines, neuroscience, oncology, and cardiovascular and metabolic diseases. The Medical Devices segment offers orthopedic products; general surgery, biosurgical, endomechanical, and energy products; electrophysiology products to treat cardiovascular disease; sterilization and disinfection products to reduce surgical infection; blood glucose monitoring and insulin delivery products; and disposable contact lenses. The company offers its products to general public, retail outlets and distributors, wholesalers, hospitals, and health care professionals for prescription use, as well as for use in the professional fields by physicians, nurses, hospitals, eye care professionals, and clinics. Johnson & Johnson was founded in 1885 and is based in New Brunswick, New Jersey.

JNJ encompasses many well-known brands, pays a good dividend, and is widely covered by major analysts, so it's easy to find news items and comments on the company and its stock. Arguably, many of its products are recession-proof, and a great deal of its business is both retail and institutional.

While 5-year gains were 75%, with dividends reinvested, that goes up to 98%. The Johnson & Johnson Dividend Reinvestment Program (DRIP) is available to registered shareholders of Johnson & Johnson and allows for the reinvestment of all or a portion of dividends into additional shares of common stock without any fees or commissions. Plan participants may also make additional cash purchases of stock up to $50,000 per year. (no commissions). There are hundreds of stocks that have similar plans, JNJ is not unique this way. DRIP's should probably be used as an easy way to automatically reinvest dividends, though most brokerage companies can arrange the same for you – and many of them do not charge for the service. I'm trying to say if the only reason you would use a company DRIP is to save on commissions, the savings are not really that much since brokerage fees to buy $50,000 of the stock are only ten dollars or less. Twenty or thirty years ago, prior to the proliferation of discount brokers, the savings were significant. Now, DRIPs are more a matter of convenience, as many of them can arrange for regular monthly contributions and to automatically reinvest the company's dividends of course. Generally speaking, a personal investor does not open a DRIP account in order to 'trade stocks'; it is more of a long-term convenience. If you need to get all or part of your money out, shareholder services and liquidate (sell) your shares and send you a check, which may take a few business days.

Facebook (FB)

The social networking company Facebook held its initial public offering (IPO) on Friday, May 18, 2012. The IPO (Initial Public Offering) was the biggest in technology and one of the biggest in Internet history.

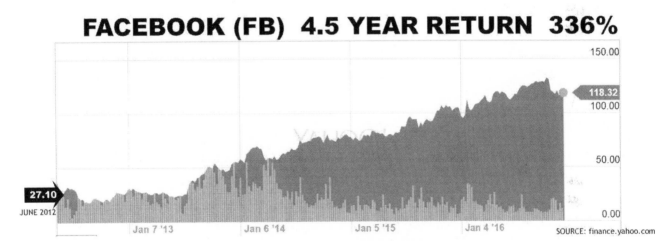

FACEBOOK (FB) 4.5 YEAR RETURN 336%

SOURCE: finance.yahoo.com

Beta: 0.41

52-Week Range: 89.37 – 119.24

PE Ratio: 45.61

Average Daily Vol 21.572 Million

EPS: $2.59

Market Cap: $341.02 Billion

Dividend & Yield: N/A

Facebook, Inc. operates as a mobile application and Website that enables people to connect, share, discover, and communicate with each other on mobile devices and personal computers worldwide. Its solutions also include Instagram, a mobile application that enables people to take photos or videos, customize them with filter effects, and share them with friends and followers in a photo feed or send them directly to friends; Messenger, a messaging application for mobile and Web on various platforms and devices, which enable people to reach others instantly, as well as enable businesses to engage with customers; and WhatsApp Messenger, a mobile messaging application. The company also develops Oculus virtual reality technology and content platform, which allow people to enter an immersive and interactive environment to play games, consume content, and connect with others. As of December 31, 2015, it had 1.04 billion daily active users (DAUs) and 934 million DAUs who accessed Facebook from a mobile device. The company has a partnership with the Federation of Indian Chambers of Commerce and Industry to augment the Millennium Alliance initiative, as well as support and expand the development of the social enterprise sector in India. Facebook, Inc. was founded in 2004 and is headquartered in Menlo Park, California. As of December 2016, they have about 1.7 billion member subscribers.

Facebook obviously is a tech / internet play. Other well-known stocks in this category are Google (GOOG), now known as Alphabet, Inc., Amazon. and Netflix. Most times the income and earnings are based on characteristics like membership, the number of users, advertising revenue/membership fees, quality of management, and new product innovations.

Twitter

In early 2014, Twitter (TWTR) stock was an IPO (Initial Public Offering) and was immediately priced over $40 per share, and the shares have plummeted to only $19.56 as of December of 2016. Although Twitter is widely known and used, the company has not been able to successfully monetize enough to drive earnings and share price upwards.

Let's pause a moment here to understand what that term *unable to monetize* means: In the case of Twitter, this business has more and more users – and continues to grow them at a good rate. But what Twitter has been unable to do, like Facebook for example, is to be able to find ways to make money with all those new users (and the old ones too). This is the case of a popular technology that has become a household name, and that seemingly more and more people use – but Twitter has performed poorly in being able to sell the ads, or in other ways, to cash-in on its own popularity. Another chief vulnerability, is that other companies have similar technology and at any time, users of Twitter can opt to use its competitors.

If you decide to buy one of the technology stocks, be sure you understand that many of these companies have special challenges. For example, many companies that were great at selling millions of desktop computers, were able to diversify their business into selling laptops, tablets, and expanding into cloud computing, or adding other services and products as technology and the public's demands change.

If there are any lessons here to be drawn for the investor, it is: 1) Just because a stock has popular services does not guarantee it success as an investment, and 2) a reminder that Initial Public Offerings, even those with great stories, can be quit risky. For beginning investors, normally IPOs, stocks without proven track records, are not advised. Remember, there are plenty of great companies with years of success, and though it is often tempting to invest in IPOs, there are often significant risks.

The Twitter IPO was in late 2013. Initially the stock was priced at $26 per share and in the first trading day rose to $45. In a few weeks, the stock climbed to over $65 and then fell to half that value by the end of calendar 2014- and has since drifted down to below $20 per share.

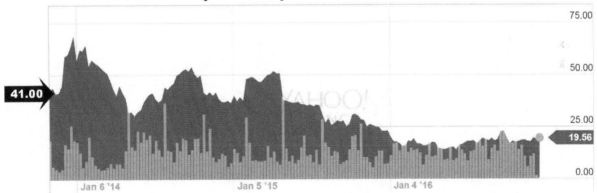

J. P. Morgan (JPM)

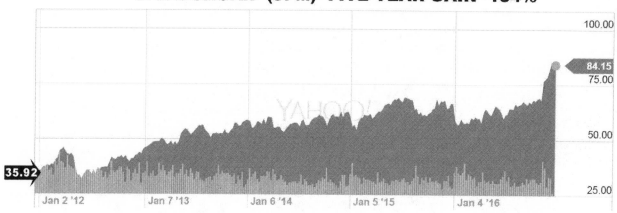

J. P. MORGAN (JPM) FIVE-YEAR GAIN 134%

52-Week Range: 52.50 – 85.79

Average Daily Vol: 17.537 Million

Market Cap: 303.16

PE Ratio: 14.36

EPS: $5.9

Dividend & Yield: 1.92 (2.25%)

Beta: 1.16

JPMorgan Chase & Co. operates as a financial services company worldwide. It operates through Consumer & Community Banking, Corporate & Investment Bank, Commercial Banking, and Asset Management segments. The Consumer & Community Banking segment offers deposit and investment products and services to consumers; lending, deposit, and cash management and payment solutions to small businesses; residential mortgages and home equity loans; and credit cards, payment services, payment processing services, auto loans and leases, and student loans. The Corporate & Investment Bank segment provides investment banking products and services, including advising on corporate strategy and structure, capital-raising in equity and debt markets, as well as loan origination and syndication; treasury services, such as cash management and liquidity solutions; and cash securities and derivative instruments, risk management solutions, prime brokerage, and research services. It also offers securities services, including custody, fund accounting and administration, and securities lending products for asset managers, insurance companies, and public and private investment funds. The Commercial Banking segment offers financial solutions, including lending, treasury, investment banking, and asset management to corporations, municipalities, financial institutions, and nonprofit entities, as well as financing to real estate investors and owners. The Asset Management segment provides investment and wealth management services across various asset classes, such as equities, fixed income, alternatives, and money market funds; multi-asset investment management services; retirement services; and brokerage and banking services comprising trusts, estates, loans, mortgages, and deposits. It has a strategic relationship with InvestCloud for the development of new digital capabilities for individual investors. JPMorgan Chase & Co. was founded in 1799 and is headquartered in New York, New York. The company has about 242,315 full-time employees.

The basic business of banking is buying and selling money. They collect deposits, then lend those dollars to customers – and make low-interest loans from the government to an extent based on deposit dollars and assets. Banks "buy" money, so interest expense is like the cost of goods sold. Banks sell money, so interest income from loans and investments represents income. For many banks, fee based revenues is a significant portion of income. Banking is undergoing additional changes, due to competition outside the banking industry, such as investment services, credit sources, charge cards, etc.; this non-interest income is increasingly important to banks. Many banks are successfully making changes to accommodate growth in online banking and this results in cutting expenses in brick and mortar offices. Generally speaking, any upturns in the economy in general result in more business for banks; conversely a shrinking economy makes bank profits more difficult.

GENERAL MOTORS (GM) FIVE-YEAR GAIN 80.5%

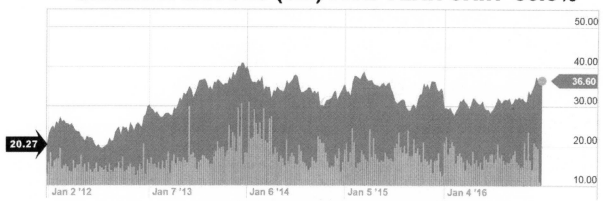

General Motors (GM)

52-Week Range: 26.69 – 37.74

EPS: $8.76

Average Daily Vol: 3.076 Million

Dividend & Yield: 1.526 (4.18%)

Market Cap: 166.4

Beta: 1.69

PE Ratio: 4.18

General Motors Company designs, builds, and sells cars, crossovers, trucks, and automobile parts worldwide. The company operates through GM North America, GM Europe, GM International Operations, GM South America, and GM Financial segments. It markets its vehicles primarily under the Buick, Cadillac, Chevrolet, GMC, Opel, Holden, Vauxhall, Baojun, Jiefang, and Wuling brand names. The company also sells cars and trucks to dealers for consumer retail sales, as well as to fleet customers, including daily rental car companies, commercial fleet customers, leasing companies, and governments. In addition, it offers connected safety, security and mobility solutions, and information technology services. The company, through its subsidiary, General Motors Financial Company, Inc., provides automotive financing services. General Motors Company was founded in 1897 and is based in Detroit, Michigan.

Picking stocks to buy and trying to judge the risks involved requires that you not only consider the company's prospects but that you do so within some context of timing. This is no understatement when it comes to examining auto manufacturers. If you were considering an investment in GM, you would want to compare it to similar companies like Ford (F), Toyota (TM), Tesla (TSLA), Honda (HMC) and others. There are also various ways to invest in the automotive industry other than only in manufacturing automobiles; there are affiliated industries that deal in everything from replacement parts (Advanced Auto Parts – AAP), to software, tires, specialized microchips, internet services, logistics, and more. Most car manufacturers have substantial international sales, so stocks prices can be sensitive to trade issues, fluctuations in currency, interest rates, and a myriad of other influences. One generalization that seems to hold true over time, and it is little more than common sense to recognize, is that a generally healthy economy carries a high volume of new car sales. At the time of this writing, the average age of a car on the road is about 12 years, historically above average. A great deal can be revealed about a stock's price behavior by using comparison charts: 1) other manufacturers 2) the S&P 500 average 3) with ancillary businesses (car parts, tire manufacturers) 4) with other sectors such as banking, technology stocks, real estate, etc. Remember, you are looking to invest in the best place that suits your investment goals. A part of that is always ascertaining risks, your personal tolerance to risk, how many similar stocks you already own (keeping in mind some diversity), and other factors. You or someone in your circle of family and friends may have a special insight into any particular market segment. Remember Peter Lynch's advice to 'invest in what you know when possible.'

Studying a stock's price (as in keeping it on your watch list for months) can often provide you valuable information about the timing of your stock buys and sales. You must be patient and willing to explore and consider many possibilities before you have enough information to gain confidence in your investments.

Another factor, and one of the reasons I selected GM as a stock example is the dividend factor; you see GM currently pays 4.18%. At present, interest rates are expected to rise over the coming year(s), but it will still be quite a while before they reach a level that approaches the amount that GM pays. You should also be aware that companies can elect to lower, raise, or stop all dividend payments without notice. For this reason, you want to study the company's history of dividend payments.

Please remember, as you read about some of the stocks I've selected for this section of the book – that I do not recommend (or not) the stocks for your portfolio – I use them here only to try and illustrate to you examples of how investors may examine and consider aspects of stocks. You may discover / determine that some of the stocks I've listed here are NOT suitable – and that is a part of learning too!

You may, over time, find a few analyst, or stock advisors that suit your style and that become a source of ideas for you. Even when you do, you are totally responsible for doing your own due diligence before putting up your money. You realize by now that if you spent an entire lifetime reading about and studying investments, you will never eliminate all risks, know everything possible, or be an investor without any poor choices ever over a lifetime. If you can't get comfortable with that idea, you might never be able to vault over your hesitation in order to take action. Action or inaction is a choice we all have to make over and over again throughout life – and our lives enjoy and endure the consequences; there is no avoiding this fact.

Did You Know: A *stock split* is a corporate action that increases the number of the corporation's outstanding shares by dividing each share, which in turn diminishes its price. The stock's market capitalization, however, remains the same, just like the value of the $100 bill does not change if it is exchanged for two $50s. These are announced ahead of time, and they can be in any increments. By the way, the historical price charts of stocks will have splits already built in to their displays. Stock splits do not change the value of your investment.

Home Depot (HD)

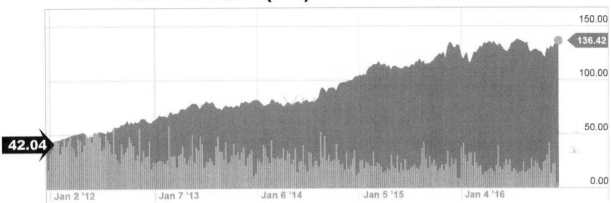

HOME DEPOT (HD) FIVE-YEAR GAIN 224%

52-Week Range: 109.62 – 139.89

Average Daily Vol: 3.605 Million

Market Cap: 166.4

PE Ratio: 22.15

EPS: $6.16

Dividend & Yield: 2.76 (2.07%)

Beta: 1.12

The Home Depot, Inc. operates as a home improvement retailer. It operates The Home Depot stores that sell various building materials, home improvement products, and lawn and garden products, as well as provide installation, home maintenance, and professional service programs to do-it-yourself, do-it-for-me (DIFM), and professional customers. The company offers installation programs that include flooring, cabinets, countertops, water heaters, and sheds; and professional installation in various categories sold through its in-home sales programs, such as roofing, siding, windows, cabinet refacing, furnaces, and central air systems, as well as acts as a contractor to provide installation services to its DIFM customers through third-party installers. It primarily serves home owners and renovators/remodelers, general contractors, repairmen, installers, small business owners, and tradesmen. The company also sells its products through online. As of December 31, 2015, it had 2,274 stores, including 1,977 in the United States, 182 in Canada, and 115 in Mexico. The Home Depot, Inc.

was founded in 1978 and is based in Atlanta, Georgia.

A great deal of Home Depot's business is by contractors, thus during cycles when homebuilding is up, so goes the stock. Compare with Lowe's Companies, Inc. (LOW).

Suggested Exercise: Use the charting service of your broker. If you don't have an account yet, use finance.yahoo.com or an equivalent website. Overlay a five-year chart that compares the gains of HD with the S&P500 index. As you will see, HD is one of those stocks that "out-performs the market."

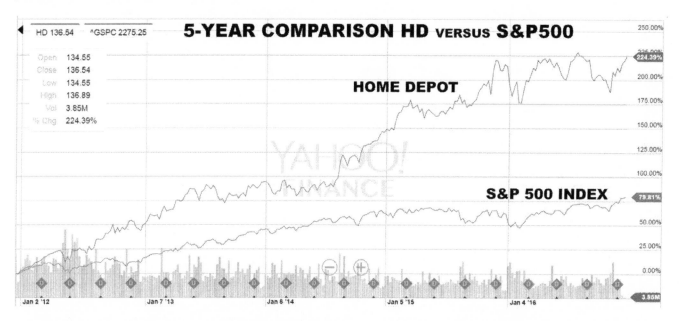

You need to learn how to use charting features to draw comparisons and arrive at your own conclusions. It is easy to compare one stock to another (like HD vs. LOW), to any index, the DOW 30 average – and to get a snapshot of how your stock has performed over time. The only way you get good at it is to practice. Our brains process visual information at more than 100 times the rate of just text and numbers, so make it easy on yourself and learn to use charting for performance comparisons. For more practice, you might try comparing your two favorite fast-food restaurants, or your bank to a competitor. Keeping it interesting is the key to learning. Instead of trying to digest raw numbers, explore ways to use charts and graphs – and you'll be able to assimilate information at a much faster pace. It also helps that you get some 'hands on' in using these graphical interfaces; you will remember much easier than merely 'reading about' doing it.

Eli Lily and Company (LLY)

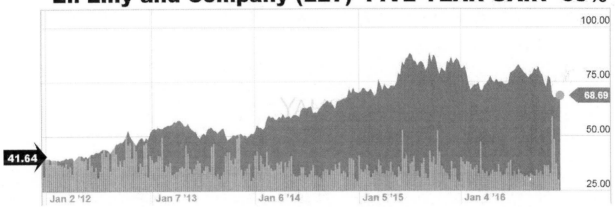

Eli Lilly and Company (LLY) FIVE-YEAR GAIN 65%

52-Week Range: 64.14 – 87.21

EPS: $2.30

Average Daily Vol: 5.47 Million

Dividend & Yield: 2.04 (3.01%)

Market Cap: 72.49 Billion

Beta: .13

PE Ratio: 29.88

Eli Lilly and Company discovers, develops, manufactures, and markets pharmaceutical products worldwide. It operates through two segments, Human Pharmaceutical Products and Animal Health Products. The company offers endocrinology products to treat diabetes; osteoporosis in postmenopausal women and men; human growth hormone deficiency and pediatric growth conditions; and testosterone deficiency. It also provides neuroscience products for the treatment of depressive disorders, diabetic peripheral neuropathic pain, anxiety disorders, fibromyalgia, and chronic musculoskeletal pain; schizophrenia; attention-deficit hyperactivity disorders; depressive, obsessive-compulsive, bulimia nervosa, and panic disorders; and positron emission tomography imaging of beta-amyloid neurotic plaques in adult brains. In addition, the company offers products for the treatment of non-small cell lung, colorectal, head and neck, pancreatic, metastatic breast, ovarian, bladder, and metastatic gastric cancers, as well as malignant pleural mesothelioma; and cardiovascular products for the treatment of erectile dysfunction and benign prostatic hyperplasia, thrombotic cardiovascular events, and cardiac ischemic complications. Further, it provides animal health products, such as cattle feed additives; protein supplements for cows; leanness and performance enhancers for swine and cattle; antibiotics to treat respiratory and other diseases in cattle, swine, and poultry; anticoccidial agents for poultry; and chewable tablets that kill fleas and prevent flea infestations, heartworm diseases, roundworm diseases, hookworm diseases, and whipworm diseases. Additionally, the company offers products to treat chronic manifestations of atopic dermatitis and congestive heart failure in dogs; chronic allergic dermatitis and kidney diseases in cats. It has a clinical collaboration agreement with Athenex, Inc. Eli Lilly and Company was founded in 1876 and is headquartered in Indianapolis, Indiana. The company employs 41,275.

The list of familiar brand names from LLY is extensive for human and animal drugs to Rx medicines and over-the-counter, to retail products that include shampoo, deodorants, soap, skincare, razors, moisturizers, sunscreen, toothpaste, toothbrushes, mouthwash, vitamins, toilet paper, paper towels, aftershaves, nasal spray, eye/ear products, antihistamines, conditioners, and much more.

As of December 2016, LLY pays just over a 3% dividend and offers DRIP with initial purchases at $1,000 and a small account setup fee of $15.00. (subject to changes of course). Eli Lilly, as with virtually all major drug manufacturers, is always under fire for drug pricing; these news stories, and stories about particular drugs (such as insulin) can influence share prices.

There is no 'right' or 'wrong' way for you to investigate and judge a stock for investment potential. Some people gravitate to the math, others do well with their awareness and common sense. Just because another investor always considers the news and earnings reports, analysts, and histories before investing in any stock – doesn't mean that's the only way to pick a stock. I know people who trade only by charting, using only what is called *technical analysis*, using software to detect patterns for pricing. Looking at a stock's price chart is not the same thing as technical trading; neither is using price charts to compare a stock's performance against other stocks or an index. Don't be in a hurry to pin yourself down to only one method; it's not a contest. Find what works for you and use the methods that make you the most comfortable. Sample all methods, and find what works best for you.

Compare AT&T (T) versus Verizon (VZ)

This comparison is between two of the major telecommunications companies, ATT and Verizon. It is very easy to compare any stock with any other, or any stock to one of the many major indexes, whether the S&P500, DOW 30, Russell, or even the price of gold, oil, or other commodity. Keep in mind, just comparing one stock's share price to another, as in this T versus VZ chart, *does not by itself directly address the potential of one stock compared to another.*

Compare Pepsi (PEP) to Coca-Cola (KO)

Now let's take two of the most widely know brands in the world, Pepsi and Coca-Cola (both trademarked names of course). The first chart illustrates the relative 5-year return percentages; this chart does not assume dividend reinvestment, only the capital gains on the stocks. By the time you read this text, the comparison will change; to get your own update, you can use your broker's charting, or go to finance.yahoo.com, put in PEP, then select interactive chart and choose to compare it with KO.

Although it is clear, that during this selected five-year period of time PEP outperformed KO in percentage return, this chart also illustrates how the relative prices of these two stocks seem to vary together (correlate) for the most part. In observing this, the chart tells you that factors other than the changes in relative value effect the prices of both stocks similarly. A chart like this can also tell you at-a-glance during what periods of time one outperforms the other. Both of these companies are known for many brands of course, not just the soft drinks that carry their names. Both companies are also very global; there are years when either of them might have greater international growth than domestic (USA). Over the years, beverage companies diversify by offering new flavors and types of beverages – depending on the demographics and flavor preferences in the countries where they have business. How well these companies evolve directly determines their continued profitability.

There is another very important yardstick to use when a personal investor is considering a stock. This illustration will also point out to you, how simply comparing *only* relative stock prices does not tell the whole story of evaluating stock performance.

The PEP versus KO chart shows that PEP stock gained 58.15% over five years. This graphic does not take into account, the total return with dividends reinvested. As it turns out, PEP stock with the choice to reinvest dividends into additional stock shares (DRIP) did quite well as you can see in the table below:

STOCK MARKET INVESTING FOR BEGINNERS

STOCK TOTAL RETURN CALCULATOR

Stock Ticker:	PEP	**Starting Amount ($):**	10000
Starting Date:	12/17/2011	**Ending Date:**	12/17/2016

RESULTS

Total Amount :	$18,303.90	**Annualized Return:**	12.84%

SOURCE: dqydj.com/stock-calculator-dividend-reinvestment-drip/

As you can see, $10,000 invested for a recent five-year period with dividends reinvested, turned that amount into $18,303.90, an annualized return of 12.84%. Here's how the KO did in the identical comparison:

STOCK TOTAL RETURN CALCULATOR

Stock Ticker: KO

Starting Amount ($): 10000

Starting Date: 12/17/2011

Ending Date: 12/10/2016

RESULTS

Total Amount : $14,121.76

Annualized Return: 7.17%

Comparing Stocks

Always remember how very easy it is to compare one stock to another. Comparisons are usually done by comparing stocks in the same group. For example, you might compare McDonalds and YUM Brands. You will find these stocks charts do not tell the whole story. YUM Brands includes Pizza Hut, KFC, and Taco Bell. You also might want to see how often each company hit its earnings projections over the last year; this can tell you something about the relative growth and consistency of each. Many times, digging into this information will merely confirm what you already know about a company. Other times, comparing the earnings and projected earnings reports might be enough to sway your choice to one stock or the other.

You recall the adage that "one bird in hand is worth two in the bush." To a beginning stock investor this advice might be sage. Although, you might be tempted to buy a stock that has a promising story of changes and innovations, it is usually more prudent to consider what a company IS doing, over what it MIGHT do in the future.

Another temptation is to buy a company's stock that is in the hole, meaning its price has dropped so much that it might be a good buy. Just remember, it could also be a company that is permanently on the down turn. If you are faced with such a choice, do some research to see why the price has fallen, make some comparisons with other similar stocks. This can tell if a whole segment (like banking, or restaurants, or oil companies) is faltering, or if it's only the company you are considering.

Another temptation is when you hear a specific company's stock price will rise because it is a candidate to be 'bought out' by another company. There can be extra risks involved in such rumored 'buyouts'. These transactions are subject to laws and regulatory approval. Other times, such offers can be withdrawn without explanation. So if you are considering buying a stock based on such rumors, that risk you are taking on might change your mind. There's another angle that comes up from time-to-time: Suppose you already own a stock, and its price has been lifted by buyout rumors. You may have a higher value stock due to this, but if that buyout does not materialize you might lose the windfall if you do not act. If this situation arises, follow the developments closely and make your decision. Often just the rumor, and not a stated fact, is enough to drive the price of a stock up. Remember, stock prices are based on perceived *future* earnings; this is the nature of the game. More often than not, these stories make little or no difference to the long-term stock value.

Don't Make Things More Difficult Than They Are

I was having lunch with a friend who is relatively new to stock investing, and he asked me, "Which do you think is better to buy, Ford or General Motors?" I immediately replied, "I have no idea but let's see what we can find out quickly." I reached for my iPad and Googled the term *Compare the stocks of Ford with GM*. In less than .47 seconds, I have just over 20 million hits on that search. Out of the first 20 or 30 results, there were reports from Nasdaq, four magazine articles, numerous comparison charts, and reports from several analysts – and they ALL were about comparing those two stocks. It isn't 1980 anymore! Instant and cheap information is at your fingertips, so don't make it difficult when you can easily find valuable information. I should warn that you *always check the dates of those links, charts, and articles* – as often the outdated ones get mixed in with current information. Of course, there is a lot of junk-information or sales pieces that try to pass for research. Just use your common sense a little and you can easily tell the difference. (It is also sometimes fun to look at the old articles to see if they got it right or not!)

Once when I was just a boy, my Grandfather told me that, when he was ten years old, he had to get up at 4:30 AM to do his farm chores and then leave for school at 6:30 AM because he had to walk six miles to school. I realized I was lucky as I could sleep until 7:30 and still make the 8:00 AM bus or ride my bicycle the one-and-a-half-miles to school and easily be on time. Now, you and I both know that it wouldn't have made me a better person if I got up at 4:30 AM and had walked six miles to school, but out of respect, I never said that to my Grandfather. The reason I mention that here is that, as a beginner in stock investing, you will hear old-timers (many who don't even use the internet) try to teach you the "old ways" of doing things. Many people who learned stock investments twenty or more years ago, choose to do things the way they learned them. Furthermore, they may carry some inherent distrust for the internet and just how easy and free it is to find valuable and useful information.

This book is all about taking the mystery out of stock investing and showing you easy, fast, and inexpensive ways to find and use good information. You are likely to encounter many investors that have done quite well using the info and technology of years gone by. They will have well-meaning advice for you and some of it will be very useful. Having said that, you do need to know that in this day and age, finding good stocks is actually a pretty easy thing to do. Of course, selecting your investments is serious work and when well-meaning people try to help, we all should be respectful as I was to my Grandfather – but you should also realize that getting up at 4:30AM and walking six miles to school probably won't make you a better person or a better investor.

I bought stocks the first time almost fifty years ago. I know the old ways, but my life-long love of technology and science has always resulted in my using the best most efficient ways I can find when investing and in all other aspects of life. I am always shocked at people of all ages who don't take full advantage of the new tools of the information age. Good and useful technology makes things easier, faster, and more simple and efficient. If it doesn't do that, then it is probably something I don't need.

Comparing Market Sectors

The following table is from: http://www.sectorspdr.com/sectorspdr/sectors/performance and may be updated from there. The table compares various sector EFTs. Seeing the relative performance over time, may help you to consider either an ETF, or allow you a way to compare one stock to its respective sector. For example you might wish to compare JNJ to the health sector, or a particular bank stock to the financial sector.

TOTAL RETURNS (NET ASSET VALUE) - MONTH END as of 11/30/2016

| Symbol | Select Sector SPDR Fund | 1 Month | Latest Quarter | Year To Date | 1 Year | ANNUALIZED | | | |
						3 Year	5 Year	10 Year	Since Inception*
XLY	Consumer Discretionary	+4.67%	+2.22%	+5.83%	+2.88%	+9.23%	+17.87%	+9.70%	+8.18%
XLP	Consumer Staples	-4.23%	-4.99%	+1.89%	+4.84%	+8.26%	+12.59%	+9.87%	+5.99%
XLE	Energy	+8.54%	+5.44%	+25.95%	+12.75%	-2.43%	+3.25%	+4.06%	+8.50%
XLF	Financials	+13.89%	+16.49%	+18.11%	+15.57%	+10.94%	+18.79%	-0.43%	+3.29%
XLV	Health Care	+1.99%	-4.67%	-3.52%	-1.81%	+9.17%	+17.12%	+9.46%	+7.48%
XLI	Industrials	+9.01%	+6.81%	+19.53%	+16.54%	+9.61%	+15.42%	+8.20%	+7.71%
XLB	Materials	+6.84%	+4.58%	+16.51%	+11.64%	+6.20%	+10.02%	+6.10%	+7.48%
XLRE	Real Estate	-3.08%	-8.40%	-1.09%	+0.93%	0.00%	0.00%	0.00%	+3.43%
XLK	Technology	+0.10%	-0.63%	+12.36%	+10.21%	+13.13%	+15.20%	+8.99%	+3.70%
XLU	Utilities	-5.38%	-4.58%	+10.59%	+12.91%	+10.94%	+9.81%	+6.34%	+6.42%

Don't be surprised if you often find individual stocks in a particular sector performing above an EFT in that sector. Picking individual stocks allows an investor to pick a top performing stock in a sector – instead of owning a basket of stocks in the sector. ETFs have fund management that charges nominal fees, which also can lower the performance a little. While small investors may opt to use an ETF since they cannot afford to own many stocks in a sector, ultimately it is they who must make the choice and bear the consequences. The so-called "safety in diversity" has a trade-off; it has a very real potential of diluting performance results. In the financial services industry, there are many people and sales materials that do not hesitate to offer "safety in diversity", without providing any specific proof of this claim. By this, I mean a direct comparison of a top performing stock in a sector to the ETF under consideration, say over a ten-year period. I have never met a company or salesperson who would offer to pay you the difference if their 'safety-through-diversity' claims cost you large profits.

It is fair to tell you that many people might challenge this advice. But it is also fair for me to point out to you that just because a statement is technically true, does not mean it is useful. For example, if I tell a man that he can have a smaller chance of his pants falling down around his ankles if he wears both a belt and suspenders, does NOT mean that the chances of it happening change significantly, or that in his lifetime the chances of it happening change much at all. *While the statement is true, it is not really useful at all.*

This next table is from: https://www.barchart.com/stocks/sectors/rankings#/
You should update from that link to get the latest version of it; note, that I chose the "10-Year" option to get a better historical view than a 1-year, or 5-year look.

Sector	Last	10 Year	10 Year Price Range	
S&P 500 Index	2,262.15	+59.49%	666.79	2,277.53
S&P 500 Information Technology	817.07	+130.66%	196.55	826.38
S&P 500 Consumer Discretionary	661.26	+118.48%	124.35	670.64
S&P 500 Health Care	804.57	+106.92%	250.65	894.36
S&P 500 Consumer Staples	535.68	+98.71%	199.28	574.63
S&P 500 Industrials	544.31	+68.12%	130.46	550.79
S&P 500 Materials	317.51	+47.04%	107.17	327.33
S&P 500 Utilities	246.47	+30.34%	113.07	269.24
S&P 500 Energy	562.03	+22.94%	299.03	738.71
S&P 500 Telecom Services	172.70	+11.06%	84.35	185.43
S&P 500 Financials	391.20	-20.82%	78.45	510.90

You'll be able to click on each segment to get more particulars and insights.

Let's examine why you might even be interested in looking at a long-term view of which sectors are outperforming others. Notice in this table from Barchart.com, that the bottom listing, S&P Financials, has the worst (10-year) performance of all. This is because the 10-year stats *include* the financial debacles of 2008, when many financial companies went belly up and/or got bailouts from the Government.

Now, I'm going to show you virtually the same comparison list but with a FIVE-YEAR perspective:

Sector	FIVE-YEAR PERFORMANCE	Last	5 Year	5 Year Price Range	
S&P 500 Index		2,262.49	+78.77%	1,248.64	2,277.53
S&P 500 Financials		390.83	+120.88%	173.43	395.12
S&P 500 Consumer Discretionary		661.27	+113.42%	306.58	670.64
S&P 500 Information Technology		816.50	+99.58%	404.37	826.38
S&P 500 Health Care		804.69	+99.27%	398.99	894.36
S&P 500 Industrials		544.56	+83.76%	285.75	550.79
S&P 500 Consumer Staples		535.50	+58.28%	328.17	574.63
S&P 500 Materials		317.78	+48.58%	205.69	327.33
S&P 500 Telecom Services		172.74	+33.69%	123.31	185.43
S&P 500 Utilities		246.47	+33.34%	170.86	269.24
S&P 500 Energy		562.36	+6.78%	376.13	738.71

Please notice that the S&P 500 Financials moved from last place (ten year ratings were -20,82%) to first place (5-year rating is #1 at + 120.88%.) This is a great example of what is called the *cyclical nature* of market segments. The drastic difference over varying lengths of time, should also remind you to always take a look at time perspectives when you consider various types of stocks. Various market segments such as financials, industrial, technical, and healthcare often display this *cyclical behavior*. Not being aware of this can be costly. Another example of this might be in considering oil stocks, or gold mining stocks; the best time to buy may not necessarily be after huge increases. When investors trade as *contrarians*, they might try to time buys at the bottom of such cycles. Even the best traders and analysts find it extremely difficult to call exact "bottom" and "tops", so be warned and don't let that "light at the end of the tunnel" turn into an oncoming train!

It has been said that the general stock market ebbs and flows over time are *the tide that rises and lowers all boats*; there is truth to this adage. There are times when perfectly good companies with widely held and traded stocks get beaten up rather unfairly (their prices driven down even though their earnings and margins have not suffered.) This is the time that investors say they are *searching for bargains* in the market, meaning stocks unjustly fallen may now be great values (ripe for buying.) You must also remember that when you think you have found such a bargain, you should be very careful. You won't find that only one or two great stocks get beaten down in an oversold market, there will likely be a great many. If you think you have found things that the general market has completely over-looked, you should think again and use caution, a lot of caution. Having said that, there are times when there are a great many opportunities in the market, whether you can take advantage is often more a matter of timing, rather than you being a top stock analyst.

Remember, there is always genius in 20-20 hindsight; there are always dozens of stock market pundits ready and willing to take credit for predicting the latest market moves. Once your name/address gets on email and mailing lists, you'll probably get lots of such false claims. A great many of these claims are made by a tactic calling *back-testing*. You might get a piece of junk mail making a claim like this one:

> *System discovered by 30-year floor-trading veteran turns $5,000 into $6.5 million in only five years!*

Back-testing is the practice of going back in time to pick winning investments and /or strategies – and it is so unethical and dishonest to present these findings as '"winning" anything. Boiler room phone sales and high pressure tactics appealing to people's greed and ambition separate people from their money everyday. Do not be one of them. There is no free lunch. Run, don't walk, but run, run, run the other way – when someone offers you something 'too good to be true.'

As I write this, there is an ad on TV on one of the major financial channels The barking ad presents:

"Chuck Hughes started trading from home with just $4,600. Within 2 years, using his own unique strategy, he made over $460,000 in profits."

They offer a free book and state that, "Last year Chuck Hughes won his 8th International Trading Championship with an annual return of 309%." Well, good for Chuck but nobody makes returns like those claimed by Chuck without taking tremendous risks; the kinds of risk that hard-earned money invested for your family's security should never visit. This type of advertising might have you believe you can do it too. This is like a lotto winner offering to sell you his/her system. There are hundreds of "Chucks" out there all humming sweet words that can separate you from your money! Remember none of the "money back guarantees" will return money you lose in investments but only the money you spend on their newsletters, stock tips, and/or other services. If you are new to investing, don't let the lure of quick and easy riches waste your money. Don't start thinking, "even if I lose a few hundred bucks, it will be worth a try." It won't! Beware of misleading phrasings and often outright scams; if they sound too good to be true, they are! They are the equivalent of investing your savings in lotto tickets. Your greatest allies are time - and the discipline to routinely pay yourself first.

Just to be clear, I never met Chuck nor have I traded his system but I do understand risk versus reward commensurate relationships - and I have common-sense. Gains like that incur enormous risks. Definitely not for beginners.

author's note: While in the Air Force, I was stationed for a while in West Texas. This is an area of the country known for colorful language and plain talk. They have a saying out there:

"Don't piss on my boots and tell me it's raining."

"If 1,000 managers make a market prediction at the beginning of a year, it's very likely that the calls of at least one will be correct for nine consecutive years. Of course, 1,000 monkeys would be just as likely to produce a seemingly all-wise prophet. But there would remain a difference: The lucky monkey would not find people standing in line to invest with him." - W. Buffett

Microsoft (MSFT)

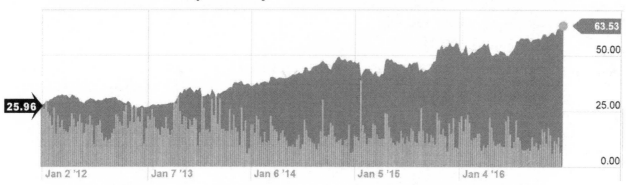

MICROSOFT (MSFT) FIVE-YEAR GAIN 144.72%

63.53

50.00

25.96

25.00

0.00

Jan 2 '12   Jan 7 '13   Jan 6 '14   Jan 5 '15   Jan 4 '16

52-Week Range: 48.04 - 64.10   **PE Ratio: 30.43**

Average Daily Vol: 28,282,318   **EPS: $2.09**

Market Cap: 493.97B   **Dividend & Yield: 1.56 (2.45%)**

Beta: 1.29

Microsoft Corporation, a technology company, develops, licenses, and supports software products, services, and devices worldwide. The company's Productivity and Business Processes segment offers Office 365 commercial products and services for businesses, including Office, Exchange, SharePoint, and Skype, as well as related Client Access Licenses (CALs); Office 365 consumer services, such as Skype, Outlook.com, and OneDrive; Dynamics business solutions, such as financial management, customer relationship management, supply chain management, and analytics applications for small and mid-size businesses, large organizations, and divisions of enterprises; and LinkedIn online professional network. Its Intelligent Cloud segment licenses server products and cloud services, such as SQL Server, Windows Server, Visual Studio, System Center, and related CALs, as well as Azure, a cloud platform with computing, networking, storage, database, and management services; and enterprise services, such as Premier Support and Microsoft Consulting that assist in developing, deploying, and managing Microsoft server and desktop solutions, as well as provide training and certification to developers and IT professionals on Microsoft products. The company's More Personal Computing segment comprises Windows OEM, volume, and other non-volume licensing of the Windows operating system, as well as patent licensing, Windows Embedded, MSN display advertising, and Windows Phone licensing system; devices, including Microsoft Surface, phones, and PC accessories; and search advertising, including Bing and Bing Ads. This segment also provides gaming platforms, including Xbox hardware, Xbox Live, video games, and third-party video games. The company markets and distributes its products through original equipment manufacturers (OEM), distributors, and resellers, as well as through online and Microsoft retail stores. Microsoft Corporation was founded in 1975 and is headquartered in Redmond, Washington.

Stock Certificates:

Before online brokers and personally-directed accounts, holding a physical stock certificate was a common way to authenticate stock ownership. This is not the case anymore. Although you may not need to hold a stock certificate, you may request one. The corporation you are holding stock in issues stock certificates, and you can get your certificate either directly from the issuing corporation or by contacting your broker who may get the stock certificate on your behalf. Not many people get or even want stock certificates as mailing it back and forth can slow the process of buying, selling, or cashing out. It is quite normal and common-place that your brokerage account authenticates your ownership.

Detailed on the stock certificate itself will be your name, the company's name, and the number of shares you own. There also will be a seal of authenticity, a signature from someone with assigning authority authenticating the certificate, and either a CUSIP or CINS number. Currently, stock certificates are seen more as collectibles and souvenirs than actual records of ownership.

Free Bonus Information from the Author

To make things easier for you. I have a **FREE PDF** file I'd like to email to you. It has many links that are in this book, so you can just "click and view" from your computer. I've also included more helpful information on DRIPS. To get the free BONUS, just send me an email to:

Don@WriteThisDown.com and put the words: BONUS STOCK in the subject line please.

I've also included a link to my blog that has some articles I've written for stock and option traders. You can send this BONUS STOCK to friends if you like.

Chapter 8: Questions and Answers

General

Question: *How much money do I need to get started?*

Answer: The moment you set aside any amount is the moment you start. It used to be common to require new account to have fixed minimum amounts, but many brokers either have waved the requirement or will if you ask. If you only have $500 just phone and explain that you will be making that initial deposit and that you have more money you'll be depositing on a regular basis after the account is open. By the way, the easiest way to fund a new account is simply do a transfer from your bank to the brokerage firm. They help people do this everyday and they are glad to assist you. If the broker you have chosen requires more than you have at this moment, no problem – just save your money until you have the minimum. The moment you set any amount aside for your new account, you have already completed the most important step; you've begun! Opening a DRIP account with a stock is inexpensive and usually requires you buy only one share of a stock to begin. This is a great way to start.

Question: *Do I pick the broker with the lowest commission fee?*

Answer: No. Almost all discount online brokers have very low fees. Whether you are going to pay $4.95 or $9.95 for your first trade is not nearly as important you finding a broker that has the software and services you will need. Most online brokers will charge $5 to $10 per trade regardless of whether you buy one share of stock or 100,000 shares. Don't let saving the price of a Starbuck's latte get between you and your ability to have a broker that suits your style and needs. Most new investors don't know this, but after you have your account open for a while, you can phone them and negotiate a better commission rate; often these discounts are contingent on a minimum number of transactions. The important thing in the beginning is that you don't let trying to save five-dollars, get in your way. Go for the trading platform you like and that suits your style and find a company that has great help-line service, so you can always be learning more.

Question: *Do I need to have my very first stock buys diversified into more than one stock?*

Answer: Plenty of people starting out only start with one stock; this isn't a problem. Better to go ahead and get started with your investing as soon as possible. If you only have a small amount of money, there's not much sense in trying to diversify yet. By "small" I mean a few hundred to a few thousand dollars. For example: If you have a thousand dollars, you probably shouldn't go to the trouble of buying $333.33 worth of 3 stocks; you'll have to pay three commissions. Over time, as you add more money and the account size grows, you will likely have other stocks you wish to add to your portfolio. When you buy a stock that pays a dividend, you may want to ask your broker if you can use the stock's DRIP. Check to see if your broker has any fees to initiate it.

Question: *Suppose I opened my new account, bought a stock, but won't have any more money to put into my account for a while. What do I do now?*

Answer: There's plenty to do. Since you've taken the right steps and your new account is now there and working for you, give yourself a pat on the back. What to do next is largely a matter of personal taste. If you are intrigued by the stock market and want to learn more about how to use your software, how to select investments, and get more familiar with the terms and the market – use the paper-trading feature of your online account to your advantage. Here's a few things you might do to learn more about your trading platform, the features your broker offers, and to practice researching stocks:

1) USE THE PAPER-TRADING ACCOUNT TO PRACTICE ENTERING ORDERS. PRACTICE BUYING AND SELLING STOCKS UNTIL YOU GET COMFORTABLE USING THE SOFTWARE (AKA: TRADING PLATFORM).

2) BUILD YOURSELF ONE OR MORE *WATCH LISTS*, AND ENTER STOCK SYMBOLS SO YOU CAN BECOME FAMILIAR WITH HOW ALL THIS IS DONE. IF YOU DON'T KNOW HOW TO BEGIN, CALL THE HELP-LINE OF YOUR BROKER TO GET STARTED. THEY HAVE HELP PAGES, VIDEOS YOU CAN WATCH, AND EVEN ONLINE FREE WEBINARS FOR BEGINNERS. OFTEN THE WEBINARS ARE RECORDED, SO YOU CAN WATCH THEM WHEN YOU PLEASE RATHER THAN HAVE A SCHEDULED TIME.

3) BE SURE TO PRACTICE READING ANALYST COMMENTS, NEWS STORIES, AND OTHER MATERIAL AVAILABLE IN YOUR TRADING PLATFORM. EVEN THOUGH YOU MAY NOT NEED ANY INFORMATION AT THIS TIME, PRACTICE SO YOU WILL KNOW HOW TO FIND AND USE THESE AND OTHER ITEMS AND PROGRAM FEATURES YOUR BROKER OFFERS.

4) REVISIT THE MATERIAL IN THIS BOOK LABELED "ABOUT WOODROW" AND THE SECTION ABOUT PETER LYNCH TITLED "INVEST IN WHAT YOU KNOW". TRAIN YOUR MIND TO THINK LIKE AN INVESTOR; PERSONAL OBSERVATIONS OFFER OPPORTUNITIES TO LEARN.

Question: *I want to buy shares of McDonalds (MCD) but the price of each share is well over a hundred dollars and I can't afford to buy 100 or more shares; what can I do?*

Answer: Through your online account, you can only buy 1 or more *whole* shares of stock. For example: You can't purchase 1.356 shares. You can however, in many cases, buy one share of a stock in a company and then purchase additional shares and partial shares though their DRIP (Dividend Reinvestment Plan). The details and fees of these plans vary from company. If you want to take a peek at how the plan works for McDonalds company, then look here: http://corporate.mcdonalds.com/mcd/investors/shareholder-information/investor_tools/how_to_buy_stock.html or HERE

Many such plans (DRIP's) allow very large commission-free purchases after you open the initial account, some allow regular monthly investments and other features to help you get started. You do not have to have a brokerage account to open a DRIP; they will set one up for you (that only handles the DRIP) for a small fee. Many of these have provisions to put your shares into an IRA, Roth, and other plans. Another way to find this information is to Google: McDonalds DRIP and look for the link there.

You are allowed to buy only whole shares of a company at your online broker but if you plan on buying more and putting in a regular amount, the DRIP may be the way to go. If you want to buy ten, twenty-five, or any number of shares, it is perfectly allowable in your online brokerage account. Remember, most DRIP's allow you to invest in more shares commission-free.

Question: *I have five or ten stocks that I think would be suitable for me to buy; how do I pick one of them to start?*

Answer: The operative word is *start*. Don't let the psychology of "buyers remorse" cause you hesitation. There is an author named Dan Ariely who has a book out called *Predictably Irrational: The Hidden Forces That Shape Our Decisions*. Dr. Ariely has created some very ingenious trials that reveal a lot about how we humans decide things. For example, if we are new car shopping and we test drive 15 types of cars, even after we make a decision and buy one of them, a part of us always wonders *did we do the right thing?* (thus: buyer's remorse) But if we lived in a land where only two cars were for sale, we might drive them both, buy one of them – and we'll be happier with our decision because we won't wonder whether we bought the right one or not. It is just human nature to second guess ourselves. There is no solution to this dilemma, so pick one!

Question: *How do I track my portfolio?*
Answer: Your online brokerage account does this automatically for you. If you enroll in a Dividend Reinvestment Plan (DRIP), you can get your current value, balance, and other information very easily online, by phone, or by mail in periodic statements sent to you.

Question: *I bought my first two stocks three months ago. I check them every day and so far I'm losing money. What do I do?*
Answer: Be calm and patient. As the old adage goes, this is a marathon, not a sprint race. If you followed the advice in this book, none of your stocks are penny stocks, and the ones you choose are tried-and-true stocks that have years of consistent performance. If you examine any long-term chart of the stock market or a particular stock, you will see that there are no "straight lines" up. Think of it as if you have planted seeds in your garden, it takes time for them to grow. Concentrate on making regular contributions to your financial savings, continue to read and learn more, but you also must have faith in the fact that regular

savings over time will pay off. Don't measure your progress in days but over months of time. If you are new to stock investing, it is quite natural for you to want to see progress, and even be a small bit nervous about your picks. Over time, you will learn that progress is not measured by days but over long periods of time.

Question: *I have selected a few stocks. How do I know when the best time to buy one or more of them?*

Answer: The short answer is: You don't! Having said that, this is a good time to discuss what it means to 'watch a stock'. As a beginner, you probably don't have a list of good stocks that you have watched over time; even the good stocks you have chosen are still unfamiliar to you in many ways. Pulling the trigger and buying your stock pick is a bit like a young couple waiting to have a child until everything is perfect – that time never comes. To state the obvious, none of us knows the future with absolute certainty. I recommend that you select a small number of stocks that meet your criteria and put the symbols in your online account's *watch list*. This watch list (and you can have as many of these lists as you want) is a feature in your account where you list stocks you wish to follow. Over time, and I mean weeks and months, as you track your investments' progress, you will also watch these stocks on your list(s). You can read the news on these stocks. You can pull up charts to see their progress (or lack of). You can follow earnings reports, dividend payouts, and other factors that help you learn the stock's behavior over time. Keep such a watch list; use it to learn about stocks that interest you. Over time you will form opinions about these stocks and become familiar with their price behavior. It is very common to kick some stocks off your list and add new ones. Over months and years, you will develop familiar favorites, and will likely buy some of them. Whenever one of these stocks on your watch lists has significant price movement (up or down), read the news on the stock, examine earnings, and other factors; this is how you gain stock trading knowledge over time. You will also notice there are times when there seems to be no explanation for a stocks price movements; this is a part of learning also.

Just so you know, there is no formula or certain amount of time you should spend watching and learning about stocks. You shouldn't assume you have to constantly watch your portfolio, and if you have chosen good long-term stocks, you won't need to do so. Many people do not enjoy this type of activity, and that's just fine. Other people who begin investing might enjoy constantly reading and learning more. Relax, think long-term with the stocks you've selected. It can be quite counterproductive to become obsessed with the daily up's and down's of your investments. In most cases, you are better off checking your account balances once a month, and remaining to abide a regular and reliable schedule of adding more money to your investments over time. Just because you have the wisdom and good sense to buy some good stocks and save money regularly, is not reason for you to have to devote a lot of time to studying and learning more. Those stocks did well before you bought them, and in most cases, they will continue to do just fine over time. No amount of worry or attention on your part will either speed them up or slow them down. If you think you need to become some investment wizard because you own stocks, forget about it; that's just not true. Stay with tried and true stocks, avoid the penny stocks, get-rich-quick ventures, hot stock tips of the day, and keep a level head and you'll be fine.

Question: *How do I know when to sell my stocks?*
Answer: Of all the questions you could ask, this answer to this one can be the most slippery of all. All I mean to say here is that there can be lots of reasons to sell a stock.

Basically, when the reasons you bought the stock are no longer there, you might consider selling it. There are instances where you may have owned a stock for years; you bought it because you felt it was undervalued and had great prospects for capital gains. Now, you see its growth has declined and you can find no proof of prospects for improvement while you do see other stocks with better chances of capital gains, dividends, and the like. An example might be you've invested in a brick-and-mortar retailer, but you find several stocks that are leaders in internet sales are making great strides of progress. Throughout history there have been companies that roll with new technology and adapt, while others do not. One of the giant companies that is a household name, Proctor & Gamble (PG), was once a simple company that made candles. Amazon started out as an online bookstore, and just a few years ago – after becoming the premier online retail behemoth – it expanded into cloud technology services and is also a world leader in that business. Staying abreast of changes in technology, consumer habits, and adapting to new opportunities can be a great way to invest.

You might need the money and choose to sell part or all of a stock.
As time passes, you may decide the grass is greener with another stock. Maybe you are like Woodrow; there's a new store in town and you can't find a parking place to shop there!

Question: *When I am buying a stock, someone else is selling it, and when I am selling a stock, someone else is buying it; what does this mean?*

Answer: Nothing! There are literally scores of reasons that people buy and sell stocks. For instance, you may be liquidating (selling) your perfectly good stock to get cash for a down payment on a home; this has nothing to do with your opinion of the stock. People cash in inheritances, sell for tax reasons, to buy another stock, or to take and protect profits. There are all kinds of reasons for buying and selling stocks that have absolutely nothing to do with whether it is a 'good' or 'bad' investment.

Question: *What are long-term and short term capital gains?*

Answer: When you buy and hold a stock for longer than a year, the proceeds (if any) are often taxed at a lower rate. At present, holding stocks less than a year, means the gains (if any) will be taxed at your regular rate. *This book is not a source for tax advice; consult your own professional and reliable sources.*

Question: *How are stocks taxed?*

Answer: When you own stocks outside of tax-sheltered retirement accounts such as IRAs or 401(k)s, there are two ways you might have a tax to pay. If your stock pays a dividend, those dividends generally are taxed at a rate of your personal income at the end of each calendar year.

If you sell a stock, you pay taxes on any profits you made over the time you held the stock. Those profits are known as capital gains, and the tax is called the capital gains tax. One exception: If you hold a stock for less than a year before you sell it, you'll have to pay your regular income tax rate on the gain. If you inherit stock shares, consult a tax professional or other reliable source about your particular situation.

Question: *What is day-trading?*

Answer: Day trading is the act of buying and selling a stock within the same day. Day traders seek to make profits by leveraging large amounts of capital to take advantage of small price movements in highly liquid stocks or indexes. Typically, day trading is definitely not for beginners, and not for most experienced investors either. It is risky and not very predictable. Day traders, should you meet one, will usually tell you about their "wins" but not-so-much about the losses they incur; like a golfer who brags about a hole-in-one but rarely mentions the tee shots that went into the woods or out of bounds.

Ben Graham, the legendary investor and Warren Buffett's teacher at Columbia has said, "You have a choice of tossing coins or taking the consensus of experts opinions. The results will be just about the same in each case." Years later his protégé, Buffett, has repeated that his teacher only had two rules about stock investing, " Rule #1 was not to lose money. And rule #2 was to never forget rule #1."

Question: *How do I find what works best for me?*
Answer: The answer to this one is a bit of a "catch-22." It's like a young person applying for their first job. They are told they need experience to get the job, but they can't get experience unless they have a job. Fortunately, picking stocks can bypass this dilemma; the solution is actually very simple. Millions of individuals, funds, and institutions own a lot of great performing stocks with which you are already familiar with. The question really becomes "how can you narrow a list of stocks down to a few that will be suitable for you?"

As much as I try to avoid sports metaphors, here is one that is just too good to pass up. This is a strike zone versus batting average chart devised by baseball great Ted Williams. In case you are not a sports fan, you should know that any player who bats four hundred (.400) in a career is considered to be an all-time great hitter. Mr. Williams was such a player.

TED WILLIAMS

.300	.320	.320	.330	.330	.315	.310
.310	.340	.340	.350	.340	.340	.320
.310	.340	.340	.350	.340	.340	.320
.340	.380	.380	.400	.390	.390	.320
.360	.390	.390	.400	.390	.390	.320
.360	.390	.390	.400	.380	.380	.310
.320	.340	.340	.330	.300	.300	.280
.320	.340	.340	.330	.275	.270	.260
.280	.300	.300	.300	.260	.250	.250
.270	.290	.300	.300	.250	.240	.240
.250	.270	.270	.260	.240	.240	.230

My first rule of hitting was to get a good ball to hit. I learned down to percentage points where those good balls were. The box shows my particular preferences, from what I considered my 'happy zone' - where I could hit .400 or better - to the low outside corner - where the most I could hope to bat was .230.

Only when the situation demands it should a hitter go outside than in; each batter should work out his own set of percentages. But more important, each should learn the strike zone, because once pitchers find a batter is going to swing at bad pitches he will get nothing else.

The strike zone is approximmately seven balls wide (allowing for pitches on the corners). When a batter starts swinging at pitches just two inches out of that zone, he has increased the pitcher's target from approximately 4.2 square feet to about 5.8 square feet. That's an increase of 37 percent. Allow a pitcher that much of an advantage and will be a .250 hitter.

Ted Williams created a stellar career for himself by knowing where pitches needed to be before he could make the best use of them – and he was rewarded handsomely for his patience. Some call this "sweet spot" their *circle of competence*. Have patience.

Here are some rule-of-thumb ideas:

1) Go with what you know. If you have experience with certain kinds of businesses that give you an edge, see if you can use your special knowledge to an advantage.

2) When you choose a stock, you will be learning more about it. The more interested you are in the subject matter, the more enthusiasm and energy you will have to study it and follow its performance and related news stories.

3) Not everyone likes to read and digest numbers. If you are good at math and enjoy it, you will be inclined to analyze news and performance of a stock using those skills. If you enjoy the aspects of certain types of businesses like electronic gadgets, computers, or phones, it may be that you enjoy keeping abreast of news on such stocks. There are people with intense interests in subjects like video gaming, and know which companies are better at producing and selling them. Almost everyone has experiences and knowledge about something.

4) It is always interesting to talk with other investors. What stocks do they own? How long have they owned them? What do they like/dislike about them? Ask when was the last time they bought more, or sold it, or switched from one stock to another?

5) Many people prefer stocks that pay a good dividend. Some people think of dividend paying stocks as "making money while they are waiting for the stock price to rise"' Be sure to gauge a stock's valuation based on historical stability and volatility, not just on the amount of dividend it pays. Compare other stocks in the same category that also pay a good dividend. Don't forget to see if such a stock has a DRIP available, either directly to the company or through your broker.

"You may have a lot of feelings about a stock, but remember the stock has no feeling about you." – W. Buffett

Did you Know?

You can have as many accounts as you want at one broker, or at any number of brokers?

You are allowed to set up a Self Directed IRA (or other type of tax-deferred account) and be in charge of your funds? If you leave a company and have a tax-deferred account balance, you are allowed (in most cases) to transfer it to your own (custodian) broker. Except for nominal transfer fees, there should be no charge for this. There are limits on how much money you may contribute to these tax-deferred accounts, but there is no limit on how many different IRA's you may have. It is also possible to set up a tax-deferred account for precious metals like gold and silver. For tax guidance, consult a professional.

Tax-Deferred Accounts, by law, must have a *custodian. A custodian is a financial institution that holds customers' securities for safekeeping to minimize the risk of their theft or loss. A custodian holds securities and other assets in electronic or physical form.* There are custodial accounts for minors (not tax deferred) where a parent or guardian is the custodian. If the account is on behalf of a child (minor), taxes are paid according to the child's rate, not the custodian's.

You may authorize a transfer of your account from one bank, fund, or broker to another. For example if you are a) changing brokers and do a total transfer, and/or b) if you are doing a partial transfer from an existing account to open a new account, or just to pass funds from one account to another.

For more details on these and other subjects, call your broker's customer service for information.

Most News is Noise, Not News

When you hear 'stock news' and feel you need to do something, come back and read these sage words from Warren Buffett:

"There is no shortage of financial news hitting my inbox each day. While I am a notorious headline reader, I brush off almost all of the information pushed my way.

When it comes to financial news, I would argue it's more like the 99-1 rule – 99% of the investment actions we take should be attributed to just 1% of the financial news we consume. Most of the news headlines and conversations on TV are there to generate buzz and trigger our emotions to do something – anything!"

> *"Owners of stocks, however, too often let the capricious and often irrational behavior of their fellow owners cause them to behave irrationally as well. Because there is so much chatter about markets, the economy, interest rates, price behavior of stocks, etc., some investors believe it is important to listen to pundits – and, worse yet, important to consider acting upon their comments." – Warren Buffett*

"The companies I focus on investing in have thus far withstood the test of time. Many have been in business for more than 100 years and faced virtually every unexpected challenge imaginable. Imagine how many pieces of gloom-and-doom "news" originated over their corporate lives. However, they are still standing.

Does it really matter if Coke missed quarterly earnings estimates by 4%?

Should I sell my position in Johnson & Johnson because the stock has slid by 10% since my initial purchase?

With falling oil prices reducing demand for some of GE's products, should I sell my shares?

The answer to these questions is almost always a resounding "no," but stock prices can move significantly as these matters arise. Financial news outlets also need to blow up these issues to remain in business."   -- Warren Buffett

Chapter 9
The Value of an Education in Compound Interest

The example in this small chapter is, unfortunately, not something we can actually do, but it does feature some valuable information about the real value of time and compound interest. After mortgage debt on homes, student loans are the second largest category of debt in the United States. A lot of people are reevaluating how they spend dollars flagged for education.

Millions of people around the world are clamoring to move to the United States because of our freedom and financial opportunities – and yet almost 75% of our families live paycheck to paycheck! The problem isn't that Americans are not smart; we are plenty intelligent. The problem isn't that we don't work hard. Millions upon millions of us work very hard every day making the most honest and sincere efforts to support our families. It makes no more sense for you to learn 40 years of economists' jargon than it does for you to drive a mule and wagon. When you consider the drastic changes in banking, shopping, and communications over the last ten years, it's easy to understand why now is the time individual investors have more power to achieve financial independence than any time in history.

"Through stupid decisions, we put half our talent on the sidelines."- W. B.

According to the National Center for Educational Statistics, the United States spends about $12,296 per student each year for elementary and secondary schools (2015 stat WSJ article). This means a high school graduate has received an educational funding of about $150,000.

Now, what comes next will likely totally shock you:

If you took just two years of the cost of that public education, a total of (2 x $12,296) $24,592 and invested it in the company that brings us Happy Meals, McDonalds - in May 2003, by the time the student graduated high school in June of 2016, it would have been worth a cool $193,545.26 (dividends invested.)

STOCK TOTAL RETURN CALCULATOR

Stock Ticker: MCD	**Starting Amount ($):** 24592
Starting Date: 08/30/2003	**Ending Date:** 06/11/2016

[Calculate] [Reset]

RESULTS

Total Amount : $193,545.26	**Annualized Return:** 17.50%

source: https://dqydj.com/stock-return-calculator-dividend-reinvestment-drip/

If our new 'high school grad' was 18 years old and invested her $193,545.26 at 10%, her future financially speaking would be quite bright. At 10% money doubles ever 7.2 years:

Money Invested at 10% Doubles Every 7.2 Years	
Age	Amount
18	$193,545.29
25.2	$387,090.58
32.4	$774,181.16
39.6	$1,548,362.32
46.8	$3,096,724.64
54	$6,193,449.28
61.2	$12,386,898.56
68.4	$24,773,797.12

Throughout this book, common sense is the constant companion of sound financial guidance: When some investment guru wants to sell you his time-tested, sure-fire "system" for $500 to $2,000, don't you ever wonder why he needs the money? Doesn't it seem totally illogical to you that someone who can make all the money he or she wants needs another five-hundred dollars from you?

Chapter 10
The Most Common Mistake in Trading

This is a no-brainer and you already know all about it, but it might be good for you to hear it again – that's up to you. The most common mistake in trading is also the most common mistaking in living. We take our profits too quickly and let the losses run until we lose a lot. This is not only the worst mistake of investors but also the most common – and one of the hardest habits to cure. If you want to avoid it and you don't have an iron-strong self-discipline and a photographic memory – then you need to learn to apply discipline to your trading. This means keeping notes and records of how you are doing, so you can look at the results somewhat objectively. Doing this without fail will help you learn faster with fewer mistakes. I know some traders, and I have done this myself, who make notes in the margins about "what they were thinking" as they chose and placed a trade.

The reason for this most common mistake is that we must admit we were wrong to close a trade that we probably thought was a sure winner. We are put in a position to disagree with ourselves, a position that all of us naturally try to avoid. This is self-denial at its worst; we must remember everyone has losing trades, disappointing trades, and there are times we don't recognize our mistakes until we have already entered a trade – and then irrational thinking can take over and increase what would have been tolerable losses. Every great warrior with a long career knows he or she has to sometimes retreat to be able to fight another day. Keeping your money is just as important as making it. We normally like to think of ourselves as having a positive outlook and a life full of hope. Not learning to cut your losses, admit when a trade isn't working, and accepting the fact that you can't control everything - can lead to the quick end to your trading. Insisting on being hopeful on trades that go wrong - is a very bad habit – and it gets very expensive.

A disciplined trader knows when to exit a trade. One of the most wonderful things about trading is that it is solitary and we live and die on our own wits; that is also the worst thing about trading. Without discipline, very few traders are lucky enough to survive. Making smart trades is half of investing; the other half is learning to keep what you make. If you are investing for your long-term welfare, you probably shouldn't be trading that often, Invest in good businesses and then hold on for the ride.

Determine Your Risk Tolerance

Another very common mistake is doing what poker players called "playing scared." Each of us has a risk tolerance, a point at where we begin to allow the fear of losing to dominate our decision making. When we begin to obsess over daily gains and losses, it is easy to lose sight of the fact that it takes time for investments to materialize the type of growth we expect. You don't find any straight lines upward in any of the stock charts; the markets just do not work that way. You have to learn that setbacks are a normal part of growth. Here's a clever graphic that I stumbled upon that illustrates a lot about life and investing: It is normal to become apprehensive about your investment choices from time-to-time. You will need to

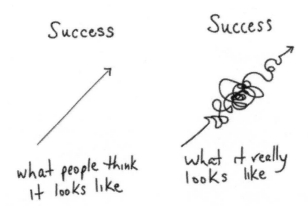

remind yourself that a degree of balance in your expectations will serve you well. Don't expect to always find 'a reason' that your stock goes up and down each day; it's impossible. Think in terms of stock prices moving in longer term trends. Even the best of companies can have a poor quarterly report. Sometimes net earnings might decrease for reasons that mean more growth over the longer term; for example a company spends a lot for expansion, or new technology, or even acquisitions that can enhance its earnings potential.

If you do find yourself unable to abide the ups and downs, perhaps you are the type of person who prefers to invest in stocks that pay regular dividends – and then have those dividends each quarter credited toward buying more shares of the stock (DRIP's).

Be mindful of your investment strategies and behavior over time. I have met new investors who always think that no matter which stock they buy, the grass always looks greener. This type will often pull out of a good stock and put the money into another stock that seems to perform better. You may need to do this from time to time, but if you form a pattern of regularly doing this, it can be caused by impatience. Impatience can drastically stunt your success.

A Parable: The Seed

An old fable relates the story of the student who was given a task by his guru. The teacher handed the young man a seed and instructed him to care for it and plant it. His instructions were to place it in fertile soil to grow, and to select an ideal location with neither too much sun nor too much shade. He was to water it daily, and to make sure that weeds did not take it over. Eager to please, the student did exactly as his teacher had instructed. Several weeks passed before he was summoned by his teacher to report on the progress of his planting.

The teacher asked if he had found a suitable fertile location in which to plant the seed. The student assured his teacher that the seed was indeed planted in an ideal location with fertile soil, a place with not too much sun nor too much shade. The teacher asked if the boy had given the plant proper care. The student described how he watered the seed every day and pulled up any weeds that were growing near the plant.

"Then tell me, how is the seed growing. Do you see what kind of plant comes from the seed I gave you?" said the teacher.

"I am sad to say," answered the boy, "that after weeks of care the seed has not grown. It is still in the ground and nothing has developed from it."

"And why do you think that is?" asked the teacher. The young student felt as if he had failed, and he even wondered for only a moment, if his teacher had given him a bad seed to teach him some lesson.

After a period of uncomfortable silence, the boy assured his teacher that every effort had been made to care for the seed properly. The boy said, "Teacher, I even dug up the seed every single day, so I could measure its progress."

"And what have you learned?" asked his teacher.

Sometimes You Just Get Lucky

Years ago, my sister came to me and told me she just got some unexpected money, the sort of mad money that you can use to splurge a little. She asked me if I knew a stock where she could take a couple of thousand dollars and make a profit. She was not a stock trader or even a regular investor in the stock market. After making her promise me, she wouldn't get upset if she lost it all – I told her I was thinking of buying a small drug company stock. I had read they were testing a new drug on some Navy volunteers that could pay off big if the results continued to be good. The stock was only about $8.00 a share, so we each bought a couple of hundred shares of it. This was over twenty years ago; the stock doubled in less than a week! I could find no explanation for it and I only guessed that there must have been some publicity about the stock that attracted other speculators and the price took a very unexpected pop up. I sold my shares immediately, and then phoned my sister as fast as I could and told her to do the same. Our $1600 had become $3200 in only four days.

My own view was that I had just gotten lucky. I knew how very, very rare it was to have a stock double in only four days. When I bought the stock, the best I ever expected was to make maybe 30 to 50% within a year – and that was extremely optimistic. So when it doubled almost immediately, I thought to myself "thank you" rolled my eyes to the sky and then took the profits as fast as I could. So I when I phoned my sister and said, "The damned stock doubled in four days, call your broker right now and sell it! Take the money and run."

I thought my sister would be very happy and would think I was a genius, but her reply absolutely shocked me. She said, "Oh no way! It just doubled. I'm certainly not going to sell it *now*." I pleaded to her that the 'worst thing can happen is that we have doubled our money' – but she was sure we had a tiger by the tail and no way she would sell it.

The stock did go up another two dollars a share the next day, but the following week the price plunged down to below $4.00 a share. A news story came out that the clinical trials were terminated because two of the servicemen in the test had gotten very sick from side effects.

I had experience trading stocks – so I knew how rare and remarkable it is to double your money in under a week; my sister did not. She was disappointed of course and losing that little bit of money didn't have any real effect for her. But I did add a new rule to my own list of stock tips: *Sometimes you just get lucky. Take the money and run!* Back then a bank savings account was paying about six percent, so (use the rule of 72) the money would have taken 12 years to double in a bank savings account. I asked my sister if she would take her original money out so she could at least break even. She declined.

Just so you know, any stock trader that can make more than 10 or 12% in a year is considered to be very successful. Here's an excerpt from Investopedia.com:

> *According to historical records, the average annual return for the S&P 500 since its inception in 1928 through 2014 is approximately 10%. However, that number can be very misleading. If an investor thinks that translates to just putting money in the S&P 500 Index and watching it double about every 10 years, he is likely in for a rather big disappointment. Accurate calculations of average returns, taking all significant factors into account, can be challenging.*
>
> *The S&P 500 is a collection of 500 stocks intended to reflect the overall return characteristics of the stock market as a whole. The stocks that make up the S&P 500 are selected by market capitalization, liquidity and industry. Companies to be included in the S&P are selected by the S&P 500 Index Committee, which consists of a group of analysts employed by Standard & Poor's. The index primarily mirrors the overall performance of large-cap stocks. The S&P 500 is considered by analysts to be a leading economic indicator for both the stock market and the U.S. economy.*

The Enemies: Greed and Fear

The enemies of patience are greed and fear. If you trade stocks, there will come a day when something like this will happen: Your investments are doing well and you are gaining confidence in your stock choices. Then, one day the DOW average will plummet by a few hundred points and all the TV news and internet stock gurus are touting ideas predicting nothing but doom and gloom for those in the stock market. My advice, short of you finding some very unusual and terrible news about your particular stock(s), is for you to start shopping for some stock bargains to buy – maybe even buy more of what you already own. Many investors, and you may be one, do not enjoy watching the market news, nor do they consistently do research to find good stock buys. If that is you, you are just fine. Just relax. Rarely do kneejerk reactions to market fluctuations advance your cause. It really isn't a matter of 'if' that will ever happen, but just 'when'.

Almost all of the talking heads on the financial channels have very short memories, nor do they measure their words very carefully. I heard major network newspersons refer to a 50 point drop in the DOW 30 average as 'a drastic downturn in today's major markets.' A 50 point drop in a DOW of 20,000 is only .25%. That would be like the value of a dollar dropping from 100 cents to 99.75 cents, and that much variation, keeping in mind that markets go up and down more than that each day very commonly, is hardly worth a news headline. The DOW average can often go up or down 5 to 10% in a few months.

The less experience you have, the more sensitivity you'll have to fluctuations in the market, your stocks' value, or other fantastic claims in the media about the stock market. The only cure for you reacting this way, is time. Over time, you get used to hearing such news and you get immune to most of it.

Here's a headline from 2009:

The **Dow** Jones Industrial Average closed at its **lowest** level in over six years on Thursday, having lost 1.16%, or 89.68 points, bringing it to a level of 7,465.95. It had, at one point, set an intraday bear market **low** of 7,447.55.   Feb 20, 2009

I had lots of friends who lost up to half or more of their retirement accounts in the financial debacles of 2009. Since that day on February 20, 2009, the DOW average has recovered to near 21,000, an increase of almost 300%. Many of my acquaintances told me how the fiasco had wrecked their plans for retirement – and as a result of that they exited, sold all their stock holdings and took tremendous losses – only to have come to regret it just two or three years later. The 'fiasco' turned out to be one of the greatest buying opportunities of all time.

Of course there were many baby boomers that had money in the stock market and had intended to retire that year; they were devastated. Financial advisors, if you didn't know, advise people close to retirement age to divest from growth stocks to securities favoring income producing instruments, such as safer dividend-paying stocks or bonds. Conversely, and quite correctly, these advisors state that younger investors who have 15 to 20 or more years to go, can afford to hold more growth stocks – and they site the reason as 'they have plenty of time to recover from any drastic drop in stock prices.' Generally speaking, this is all sound advice.

I get a lot of communications (mostly emails) from people who read my books or articles, and a great many of them are either already retirement age, or within five or ten years of it. Many of these, due to the opportunities in the stock market, choose to take their chances with stock investments. One of the reasons for this is that 30 year CD rates are only about 3%. This means for each $100,000, they would receive about $3000 per year, so a half a million dollars in a retirement account drawing interest only would produce a meager $15,000 a year income. One can easily argue that with the annual inflation at about 2%, the buying power of that annual stipend will continue to decay. Back in 1978, when home mortgage rates were commonly 14% or more, bank CD rates were as high as 18%. Imagine, having CD's that double in value every 4 years! (rule of 72) Of course inflation was wildly high back then; in 1979 it was 11.22%. Using the rule of 72, this means ones savings back then would devalue in spending power by 50% in only (72/11.2) six and a half years! That makes the current inflation of about 2% look pretty good!

You will discover that every generation and every demographic (boomers to millennials) has its own challenges. Through all of this, you must remember the individuals that prospered the most were the ones who invested regularly in order to build themselves a second income.

On Greed: There an old adage among grifters and scam artists: *You can't con anyone who isn't greedy.* My favorite antithesis to this is: *If something sounds too good to be true, it probably is.* We usually think of ways a scammer could use our greed against us, but we must also consider our own self-control and discipline as a countermeasure to our internal greed. Without this internal control, we are susceptible to internal emotions that might skew our decision making. I can't count the times I've have friends who tempt me to buy penny stocks; those cheap unproven shares that don't even trade in a known market like NYSE or NASDAQ, but they are only listed in the "pink sheets." Just last week, one of my friends who is rich enough to burn money in his fireplace, gave me a hot tip on a penny stock. "I bought it for only $0.0375 a share and in two weeks it's up to 8 cents a share. It's more than doubled already." To tempt me even more, he tells me about how last year, he made twenty grand on a five-hundred dollar investment in another such stock.

These types of stories do what I call "tugging at our lotto money", that small amount of mad money that we think we'll never miss even if we lose it all. There is no way a chance to make that kind of return is not subject to extreme risk. If you think most people would never pay good money for such wild unlikely chances of winning, think again. There is something in the human DNA that is a drive to take chances, when the payout is perceived to be almost life-changing. This is why lotto ticket sales amount to billions a year, over $70.5 billion in fact! The truth is that lotto tickets are a sort of tax on people who are bad at math!

The attraction of lotto tickets and penny stocks is that it feels good to own them, even though you are almost certainly going to lose a small amount of money and you know it. I suppose the payoff of these losing propositions is a small amount of fantasy mixed with a hit of endorphins or serotonin. Just so you know, I have nothing against anyone buying a lotto ticket or a penny stock; I only have a problem when someone calls it an 'investment'. Sooner or later, you will have a friend or acquaintance come to you with a "hot stock tip" that will set you up with dreamlike profits. If you are seriously tempted, just take a dollar bill out of your purse or wallet and burn it – and then think again. It will be a cheap lesson!

In any quest for *Paycheck Freedom* or a longer term savings plan, you must be motivated, relentless, and focused. Use that determination to build your freedom. Executing your plan is not sacrificing anything; it is winning your life from day-to-day financial worries. The rewards will astound you. That's all it takes to be your own money genius.

Chapter 11
A BONUS for You

Free Bonus Information from the Author.

To make things easier for you. I have a FREE PDF file I'd like to email to you. It has many links that are in this book, so you can just 'click and view' from your computer. I've also included more helpful information on DRIPS. To get the free BONUS just send me an email to:

Don@WriteThisDown.com and put the words: **BONUS STOCK** in the subject line please.

I've also included a link to my blog that has some articles I've written for stock and option traders. You can send this BONUS STOCK to friends if you like.

A Personal Comment from the Author:

Here's an excerpt from an article in the *Wall Street Journal*:

The U.S. May Be the World's Richest Country, But It Ranks 14th in Financial Literacy –

"By many measures, the U.S. is the world's wealthiest country—but it's not because Americans are the best with their finances. In fact, a sprawling global survey of financial literacy around the world finds that the U.S. ranks 14th, behind Singapore and the Czech Republic."

The educational system in our country gets an "F" in financial literacy. There are pockets of people and schools that do get it right, but for the most part most people get almost no lessons at all in personal finance.

More important that any *facts* in this book, is the *factor* of any individual's motivation to start investments as early as possible.

The ads that play on TV about investments are usually financially secure older people, living in an upscale home, driving nice cars and enjoying international vacations in exotic places. The TV ads should be showing a young individual or couple working two jobs and extra hours – the everyday people who find just a normal life too expensive to even start to save for retirement. This is more close to the norm in our country.

All that TV ads offer these people - is fast food and a new car!

There are not ads telling you how to pick a good stock, how to reinvest the dividends free, and to buy stock without having to pay a commission – because nobody can make money telling you the quickest cheapest way to invest! There aren't ads teaching people about how money compounds or the *rule of 72. Nobody gets paid to do that. All the ads on TV are to get money that people already have*, not to show them how to become wealthy.

I don't mean to say that anyone without stock investments is in dire straights for money; that is certainly not true. There are lots of ways to make money, save, and invest.

But what is true is: **Only people who understand how to use money will avoid having to contend with money problems for a lifetime.**

Please consider sharing the message in this book with as many people as possible. It is my hope that hard-working, honest people get the basics on how to avoid letting money worries become central to everyday living.

We have to stop telling young people that saving for retirement is a first priority. Our society has been pumping that message out for over thirty years now and still, 3 of 4 families live paycheck-to-paycheck. The message we've been sending clearly isn't working.

The priority should be showing people how they can get what I call Paycheck Freedom in 36 to 60 months. We must give people a real tangible goal that is achievable and motivating.

John Lennon said, "Life is what happens to you while you are planning it." For us to keep sending people the message that financial security is what happens after age 65, is so wrong! This is a false narrative.

Financial security should start as soon as possible, and last a lifetime.

In closing, I want to show you this quote on intelligence I found recently. It's from Nassim Nicholas Taleb, author of *Black Swan*:

> *"They think that intelligence is about noticing things are relevant (detecting patterns); in a complex world, intelligence consists in ignoring things that are irrelevant (avoiding false patterns)"*

This quote is eminently pertinent in our junky crowded world of information overload from media and the internet. Of course it's great to get vast knowledge at almost the speed of light, but we do realize that all the trash information reaches us at the same remarkable speed and volume! In a fashion, our intelligence these days, comes from what to avoid, as much as it comes from what we gain. Unfortunately, it is becoming progressively easier for things to get dumbed-down and shortened into sound bytes of misinformation, each piece potentially an imposter for truth. In taking charge of our own education, we become more aware of which information is to our advantage. If you do not take charge of your future, then someone else will. Good luck to you. Thank you for your support. – the author

If you wish to write me with a comment or suggestion on how I can improve this book; my email is Don@WriteThisDown.com I'd appreciate your comments and I'll answer every email personally. Thank you for your support. Don't forget to put BONUS STOCK in the subject line to get your free bonus materials.

If you feel inclined to leave a good book review on Amazon.com for me, I thank you. Even the shortest of comments help me gain visibility to more readers. I appreciate your support.

If you need discounts on multiple copies for investment clubs, classes, etc. Email me for info, tell me about how many copies you will need and I will reply promptly.

Made in the USA
Lexington, KY
20 July 2019